BATTLE-GROUND

BATTLE-GROUND

A Personal Account of God's Move
Upon the American Military Forces

By Curry N. Vaughan, Jr.
Chaplain, Lieutenant Colonel
United States Army

With Bob Slosser

LOGOS INTERNATIONAL
Plainfield, New Jersey

BATTLEGROUND

Copyright © 1978 by Logos International
All rights reserved
Printed in the United States of America
Library of Congress Catalog Card Number: 78-51865
International Standard Book Number: 0-88270-301-3
Logos International, Plainfield, N.J. 07060

For we wrestle not against flesh and blood, but against principalities, against powers, against the rulers of the darkness of this world, against spiritual wickedness in high places.

—Ephesians 6:12

Table of Contents

BATTLE-
GROUND

1

BLACK MONDAY

"Bravo Lima! Bravo Lima! This is Bravo Lima!" The radio squawked more than it talked. "We're surrounded on all sides! We've been cut off—"

Silence.

A half dozen of us clustered around the radio in the chilly dampness of dawn. We stared at it for several seconds, and looked from face to face. The company commander's features were hard and white under his dirty green helmet. What was happening?

The radio crackled again. Our eyes sprung to it in unison. "This is Firefly. Fire concentration nine. It's our only hope. Fire concentration nine!"

Silence.

The whole world was silent. Not a breath was heard; not a scrape or scratch. Could an entire infantry platoon—our guys—in the jungle of Vietnam be instantly cut off from the whole world? What had happened?

Twenty-four hours earlier it had been Easter morning. As

chaplain of the Third Battalion, 173rd Airborne Brigade, I began that day in joy and expectation, ministering the good news of the resurrected Christ to one thousand men in the jungles, swamps, and hills of South Vietnam.

The sun was ready to burst over the deep-green horizon as I spoke the opening words of the sunrise service. "Lord, we come together in your name on this beautiful morning, and we praise you. . . ."

A hundred men in our base camp area bowed their closely cropped young heads in a semicircle around me. The morning was bright, and the sky a glistening pale blue, bouncing lightly off the tropical greenness of the forest. The colors were like those of a fairyland—bright, exaggerated.

The men held the little leaflets I had obtained from the chaplains' corps and read solemnly and sweetly the responsive readings for that special day. Dressed in green fatigues, just as they were, except for my long black stole with the golden crosses at the bottom, I read my solo lines with gusto, glad to be with those good, young men.

Then came A Company in the open field, then the other units—all the way down to platoon size—fourteen services proclaiming the love of Christ to every unit in the battalion except for one, the First Platoon of B Company, which was on the move. As the day wore on, I promised myself I'd get to B Company early in the week.

At sunset, I led that holy day's last service, out in the field on the edge of the jungle with D Company. The sun was down and darkness fast approaching as we sang our final hymn, "How Great Thou Art." The war seemed far away as our eyes roamed over the beauty of that Asian land. We lost ourselves in the music. "O Lord my God! When I in awesome wonder, consider all the worlds Thy hands have made. . . . When through the woods and forest glades I wander . . . When I look down from lofty mountain grandeur and hear the brook and feel the gentle breeze . . . How great thou art. . . ."

The hundred or more of us weren't exactly the Vienna Boys' Choir, but we had enthusiasm and joy. I could feel my face stretching wide with a smile. The others had their own looks. Some smiled. Some were very serious, heads down. There were always thoughts of home.

"I wonder what Charlie [the enemy] thinks of all this?" I said to myself as the singing faded out over the hills and valleys of the jungle.

Night came quickly. I sat in a small group eating C rations and listened to the men talking. I had grown very close to the men in D Company for no specific reasons other than the fact that twenty or more of them had asked Jesus Christ into their lives in recent months and were attempting to follow Him as best they could. The subject of God drifted in and out of the conversation as we lounged on the ground.

"Curry." It was Ken, the company commander. "You know, days like today have really made a difference."

I looked into the shadows of his face but could see very little of his expression. I remained silent.

"This whole thing becomes a whole lot more bearable. If you can walk with God—and that's what a lot of us are trying to do—you can make it one day at a time, and do your job, the job you have to do."

As he hesitated, I nodded and spoke softly. "I believe that's right, Ken. Christ is the only one who's going to bring us through this. I'm sure glad so many of you guys believe that."

He shook his head, and looked down at the ground. "It sure makes a difference in trying to lead a bunch of men in a job like this, too." He looked back up into my face. "There are right ways, and there are wrong ways, in leading a unit. The Lord enables us to find the right way; He shows us how to get the best out of the men."

An hour later, as I curled up on my air mattress, I looked up into the starry sky. "Lord, it's been a good day, and I want to thank you for it."

I felt a hand on my shoulder, and my eyes popped open.

"Sunrise, sir." A young face looked down into mine. "We have to stand to."

I looked into the sky. It was getting light. Stand-to was a discipline imposed by Ken, a veteran of three years in Vietnam, but I hadn't experienced it before. I obeyed the young man and crawled out.

As I approached the company headquarters area, I spotted Ken. "Good morning, chaplain," he said with a smile. "Weather's good."

"Praise the Lord," I said, but my heart really wasn't in it. A hot cup of coffee might change that.

"What's your thinking behind this early morning call?" I asked, trying to bring myself to alertness.

"This is the time when a combat unit is most vulnerable to attack," he said. "The enemy can attack at sunrise with full advantage of daylight, and if the men are asleep, the attack will probably be successful."

I nodded. "Makes sense."

"We make it a practice to have each man awake and alert before dawn," he continued. "For further security, radio contact is established with each unit."

I opened my mouth to ask how that worked when the Bravo Lima distress call blared through the radio, "Bravo Lima! Bravo Lima!" I found myself not breathing. Twenty-three men were out there. And they were in deadly danger. First the radio squawked with the platoon sergeant's message, and was silent. Then the artillery liaison made his desperate call. That was the last word we heard.

"It's like a bad dream," I thought. Our area had been

relatively quiet; none of our units had been attacked in full force. But just as we talked about being prepared, this was happening. Bravo Lima was somewhere in the thick of the jungle—alone.

Then realization sank into me. *That* was Bravo Lima—the First Platoon of B Company—the only unit I had not reached yesterday with Easter services. Guilt pangs shot into my chest like arrows. "I should have made more of an effort to get to them," I said under my breath. "Lord Jesus, please help them!" All we could do was wait and think.

In a few minutes word was passed to me, "Chaplain, the battalion commander is on his way. He wants you to stand by to accompany him."

It seemed like eternity as I waited. The colonel would want to go directly to the position where Bravo Lima was thought to have been hit. D Company was alerted to move as soon as possible in pursuit of the attackers.

Slowly word was trickling in by radio from other units, but details were sketchy and uncertain. Some were alive but wounded. Many were killed. This was all I knew as I heard the commander's helicopter in the distance.

After landing, the colonel spoke softly but intensely to Ken and then motioned for me to get aboard. The air tingled with tension.

As the chopper rose above the beautiful green and tan countryside, seemingly so serene, I couldn't believe what was happening. Our men were gone. Could this be?

Before long, the helicopter began to circle. We were over the area. I strained to detect a sign of life or movement below, but there was only thick jungle. Soon radio contact was made with someone on the ground, and he stepped out into a clearing. Other troops had arrived. We circled for fifteen minutes while getting available details of the tragedy from the operations officer on the ground. There was no need for us to go down after all.

It took several hours to patch together a reliable account of what had happened. But several facts were immediately known, the starkest of which were, eleven men had been killed, twelve wounded; no one had escaped.

The men of Bravo Lima had been caught by surprise. They had not observed stand-to at sunrise. A Viet Cong force had surrounded them on three sides before attacking and had opened fire while most of our men were still asleep. Few had been able to return effective fire. The platoon sergeant had lost control and was killed even as he talked to higher headquarters by radio. The artillery liaison had been calling for "concentration nine," which would have placed a barrage of artillery right where he was. He knew it was the only hope. But he, too, had been killed as he called.

The Viet Cong had obviously moved in quickly, and only twelve Americans, all wounded, were able to retreat. Eleven had been left behind. Each of them, dead or alive, had been shot through the head by the Viet Cong as they overran the position. We would never know how many of those eleven had been dead before they were finished off with the coup de grace. In our minds, it was pure murder.

The bodies of the eleven men were returned to battalion headquarters. I looked out at the airstrip. Eleven brown canvas bags were lined up at one side of the landing area, each one containing the body of a man—a comrade—who had just a few hours earlier been alive. My throat was full and I had difficulty breathing.

As I looked around at the headquarters area, I was sharply aware of the pain, the sense of loss, on the face of everyone in sight, officers and enlisted men alike. There were no smiles; every face, every word, was dark. A depression was settling over the entire base camp.

"What *is* this?" I thought. "Men have been killed here

before." But there was something special about this, something traumatic. There was anger—yes, a deep anger about losing. We had been losing three or four guys a month, and that was tragic. But those usually resulted from booby traps or chance shots—and always in ones and twos. But this time, eleven guys were gone, and they hadn't merely been killed in war; they had been murdered. Deep depression and anger weighed upon the Third Battalion. We did not understand our enemy.

Although I felt our battalion's loss heavily, I actually hadn't known most of the slain men personally. In fact, I thought for several hours that I hadn't known any of them, but it turned out that I was closely linked to one. His name was Ken—Sergeant Ken Bird.

The battalion commander got hold of me again. "Curry, Sergeant Bird has a brother in one of the other battalion units. I want you to fly out there with me and talk to him."

As we landed in the jungle clearing, I saw one of the men running toward the helicopter. I knew it was Ken's brother. Looking into his face, I knew too that there was no need to say anything. He had already received word of Ken's death.

After a few minutes we climbed into the helicopter together. We talked about Ken, and wept. I was afraid I wasn't much help.

"He was a good guy, chaplain. And he was a good soldier. This shouldn't have happened to him."

I nodded my head, and looked at the floor of the aircraft. "I know, Bill. We don't understand these things. I wish I had known your brother better."

He lifted his head and looked into my face. "Oh, listen, chaplain, you did a lot for him. I'm so grateful for how you helped him."

I had helped him? I was startled. How had *I* helped him? Sergeant Bird. Ken Bird. How had I helped him?

Then it hit me like a thunderbolt. "Yes. Yes! Now I remember. Oh, God! I *do* remember!" Tears burned my eyes.

It had been about three weeks earlier. Ken had come to talk about some personal problems back home. I remembered how discouraged he had been. He and his wife had been having marital difficulty. We had talked and prayed, and Ken had found courage. Before parting from me, he had given his life to Christ. "Come into my life, Jesus, and take over," he had prayed. "I need you." It was a simple prayer, but the Lord had touched him immediately and given him strength to go on.

A bit of joy swept through me as I recalled those moments. I knew that Ken Bird was alive in Christ; death had had no claim on him. Though I agonized with Bill—and regretted with pain the personal loss we all had experienced—I could rejoice over the hope of the Christian. Ken had placed his faith in Christ, and he was alive even though he had been murdered on the battlefield.

At the memorial service for the eleven dead men, soldiers wept openly before the eleven rifles lined up in a row. They were unashamed. Other men in this war and other wars had seen greater losses, but this was our first big loss, and it was very great. The bugler, overcome by emotion, could hardly play "Taps."

I conducted a worship service after the memorial ceremony. Almost every man in the company jammed into the small, makeshift chapel we had set up in the tactical briefing room. We prayed and we sang, and then I spoke briefly about life in Christ. I tried to emphasize "life," not the "death" that had so flooded our senses in the last few days.

Forty men, including the tough first sergeant of the

company, remained in the chapel after the service, some to accept Jesus as their Lord and Savior, others to receive further counseling on living the Christian life. Even in the midst of great tragedy, the Holy Spirit was working positively to change lives. And I was able to see enough of those men later to know that at least some continued in their commitments to Christ, allowing His Spirit to work in them and prepare them—even in death—for His second coming.

One man, a big, burly soldier, came to me two days after the memorial service. He was a member of Bravo Lima, but because he had been sick in the hospital, he had not been with the unit at the time of the attack. When he approached me, he was weighted down—almost visibly bent over—by a sense of guilt about not having been with the unit. He clenched and twisted his rough, strong hands in front of him, from time to time bending his head forward almost to his knees in great anguish.

"I should have been with them, chaplain," he sobbed. "I might have been able to help. We were a good unit. I might have been able to help. But I let a little sickness get me down."

"Listen, my brother," I said softly. I knew exactly, from personal experience, what he was feeling. "You were not goofing off. You were in the hospital." I paused, and pressed on. "And you mustn't forget that the Lord is God. He's in control. This happened this way for a purpose, even though we may not see it right now."

He continued to twist his hands in front of him. I thought he might actually break his fingers or wrists as he clenched and twisted in desperation.

"Chaplain." He looked up into my face, and I saw the suffering in his dark brown eyes, brimming with tears. "This body is really ugly, you know." His face twisted grotesquely, and he literally pounded on his chest with his big hands. The tears spilled from his eyes. "This body is ugly, but it's what's inside that is beautiful. It's what's inside that lives."

I knew then he would be all right. He would make it.

That night, alone, I sat in semidarkness in the chapel. I was vaguely aware of movement and the sounds of life outside. But, inside, all was quiet. I was filled with words and ideas. They ran together, and eventually formed mostly questions.

"Lord." I'm not really sure I spoke aloud into the enveloping darkness. I may have talked only in my mind. "How can any good come out of all this? It seems so futile and useless."

The flood of words unscrambled into rambling thoughts. "Why did those men have to die? . . . Even those who loved you died. What are wars all about? . . . You can stop them, Lord—can't you? . . . Why, Lord? . . ."

The flood surged and crested. "Do you have any use for soldiers, Lord? . . . What do you think about people like us, people trained in warfare? . . . Are we an abomination? . . . If you love us, why do you let us go into this? . . . You surely must want something different for us. . . . Who are we, Lord? . . . What are we? . . . Should we put away our arms? . . . right now? . . . Should we refuse to fight? . . . at all costs? . . . What is it, Lord? . . .

Few answers came that night. But as I talked and spewed out my confusion and uncertainties, I drifted and eased into a mysterious peace. I *knew* I was not alone in the chapel. I *knew* my challenges were not improper. I *knew* my Father understood.

"Lord." I'm quite sure I spoke aloud this time. "I know I'm toying with your sovereignty and justice. But there's just so much I don't understand, and I feel so inadequate. We've had a terrible tragedy here with these men—and I just don't understand."

I stopped for nearly a minute, and listened to the silence. Even the outdoors seemed quiet. "They were all so young, Father. But I guess . . . I guess if they had died at forty, sixty, or a hundred years, they would still have to die . . . and compared to eternity, the difference is really insignificant. . . . Yes, Lord . . . it's what we do with those years, isn't it? . . . That's what counts."

The night was very silent.

2

THE BEGINNING

I slouched in the pew and let my thoughts run. They wouldn't stay fixed on the chaplain in the pulpit. He was talking about God, naturally, but it seemed like mostly old stuff—Jesus, His life and death and resurrection, the fact that He was the Son of God. I'd been hearing that for as long as I could remember; I was eleven years old.

The man in front of me was really tall, and he sat very straight. But, come to think of it, all the men sat very straight—their women, too. We were in the Protestant chapel at Fort Knox, Kentucky. My dad, an army officer, was stationed there; the Korean War was in full rage. It wasn't a bad place, as army posts went. Old and historic, it was situated in a beautiful part of the South, a bit more than thirty miles southwest of Louisville. A lot of exciting things went on there. Gwynn and I lived a good life, although we had moved around a lot. He was my younger brother, sitting on the other side of dad and mom. Mom held my baby sister, Clara.

It was the regular Sunday morning service, and things were comfortable. But the chaplain seemed to be building up to something. His voice had become deep and soft. What was he saying?

"Have you ever accepted Jesus Christ into your life as your personal Savior?"

I had a very logical mind as a youngster; I was able to examine things rather detachedly. The chaplain's question, for some reason, fascinated me. "No," I finally said to myself after examining everything closely and calmly. "I have never accepted Jesus Christ as my personal Savior." I sat still for a moment. "I'll have to do that sometime." I believed in God fully. It seemed that He had presented himself to me from the very beginning and my child's mind found Him quite logical. If He wanted me to accept Jesus Christ as my "personal Savior," that's what I'd do.

It was sometime after nine o'clock that night. I was alone in my room and in my pajamas. The weather was unusually warm, sultry, and I remember that the outdoors seemed very quiet.

I knelt beside my bed and placed my elbows on it, cupping my chin in my hands. I was very methodical—and honest. "God." I spoke the name without qualms, unashamedly—logically. "I don't exactly know what this means, but I accept Jesus Christ as my personal Savior." It was as simple as that. Whatever I knew or did not know about the Bible and about Christ himself was of no concern to me or to God. I had asked Him into my life and He had responded. I was born again.

Gwynn and I were playing hide-and-seek in the attic of our three-story home at Fort Knox. It was winter and the weather was cold; a light snow had covered the ground. Several weeks had passed since my acceptance of Christ.

It was my turn to hide. I studied the attic. We'd tried just about everything there. "I've got it." I snapped my fingers lightly. "I'll hide out on the roof."

It was tile, and very steep. An attic window opened right onto it, and I was able to get out and work my way up. "Shoot! The noise is giving me away!" I whispered, but I knew the game was up. I was slipping and scraping on the tiles.

Gwynn stuck his head out the window. "Hey, what are you doing?"

"I'll be right down," I said.

"Do you want me to help you get back in?"

"No, I'll make it."

I was confident. Cautiously I moved down beside the eave protruding from the steep roof, holding onto the tiles at the edge of the eave. Suddenly a tile pulled loose, and then another. I felt myself sliding. It was so slow. I was just barely slipping, but I couldn't stop. There was nothing to grab. Everything was quiet, and in slow motion. I simply was sliding toward the edge of the roof. I tried to stick my foot into the gutter, but missed, and I fell. I plunged thirty-five feet to the concrete roadway below, but remembered nothing after slipping past the gutter.

The bright lights of the emergency room blinded me and I was unable to open my eyes beyond mere slits. But I was awake and aware that people were doing things to my clothes, moving their hands around my body. They were cutting my clothes off! I remembered that clearly. Then I lost consciousness.

Everything was dark when I woke again. Oddly, I knew where I was—a hospital room. The only light was coming through the door. I could hear soft noises outside the door— people moving quickly in rubber-soled shoes—squeak squeak, squeak squeak. But I was alone, and surprisingly lucid for just a few moments.

All I remembered was that I spoke tearfully into the darkness. "Oh, God, please help me." I could feel the tightness of my body, like an overinflated inner tube. I had a sense that I was oval shaped, like a football. Everything hurt. But that's all I remembered as I slipped into unconsciousness again.

Several days went by, and the tightness of unknown internal injuries continued. Then, very quickly, the tightness subsided, and my name was removed from the danger list. My parents were overjoyed. All Gwynn did was smile all over his face. He had been scared.

I had cracked my pelvis, among other things, and it healed extraordinarily rapidly. But one serious problem remained. My left wrist had been so badly broken and mangled that the doctor said it would not heal. My left arm would always be two or three inches shorter than the other.

The weeks sped by, and late one afternoon, the doctor spoke again to my parents. He had been with the specialists. "Your son's wrist has improved steadily," he said. "Our prognosis was wrong, apparently. The arm and the movement are becoming more and more normal."

I looked at my mother, then at dad. I just smiled. God had answered my prayer. He had healed me. It was all very logical.

I was a freshman in high school and active in the Boy Scouts. Aiming toward the God and Country Award, I was assigned to work on certain requirements with an army chaplain—Chaplain Helt. He was a kind and dedicated man who always seemed to find time for me no matter how busy he was. I was impressed.

It was during a Sunday service in the hospital, where a friend and I assisted Chaplain Helt as part of our duty to the community, that I had my first thought about becoming a chaplain. I watched him—a short, heavyset man in his mid-thirties, quiet and serious as he ministered to the needs of the suffering.

"Someday I'm going to be a chaplain," I said, just ever so audibly as I watched. I was a lot like a little kid seeing a train engineer and declaring that he was going to be an engineer when he grew up, or a jet pilot, or a football player. But I meant it at that moment. And the idea just sort of hung around.

Then came the time of choice. I was a senior in high school, having been sent to Castle Heights Military Academy in Lebanon, Tennessee, to finish up. For no clear-cut reason, I decided to read the Bible that year, and before long had completed the New Testament. That experience set a strong current in motion in my life right at the moment I was grappling with the selection of a career.

The military pulled strongly, of course. My dad's army career had been immensely satisfying to all of us, and I was quite happy at a military school. I was a good ballplayer, definitely the infantry, airborne, ranger type, and the prospects looked good. But I still felt a surprisingly strong tug toward the ministry. That freshman remark had lingered. In fact, in the last few months, the thought had moved into the mainstream of my consciousness.

"You're kidding," I said to myself one day. "Ministers are nice, easygoing guys with good speaking voices." I laughed. "They carry Bibles around, and sit with their hands folded in their laps, and say nice things all the time."

I was coarse and muscular, fast approaching six feet and a hundred ninety pounds, a hustler, frequently loud-mouthed, and more than a little troubled by a bad temper and loose tongue. I could blow up at the drop of a hat.

"You're kidding," I repeated. But I didn't laugh any more. "No, I'm not," I said at last. "I'm not kidding. God is calling me into the ministry." I would satisfy my natural instincts toward the army—I'd been sold on that branch of the military ever since watching West Point play football on television—and my spiritual yearnings toward the ministry by combining them. I'd aim at the army chaplaincy.

Right away, I made my intention public, and my friends at

Castle Heights had a hard time swallowing it. It didn't fit my image. "Curry," said one of my football teammates, "I just can't see you in the ministry."

I smiled. I was having a little trouble with that myself.

The next hurdle was cleared when my appointment to West Point came. I accepted it without hesitation. My plan was laid: after winning an engineering degree, I'd serve the required four years on active duty as an officer, picking up some additional education in assorted training schools around the world. Then I'd start worrying about preparing for the chaplaincy. I prayed about it, and was comfortable with it. God would work something out.

Leaving my family at Fort Stewart, Georgia, I flew by commercial airliner into the sprawling, smog-shrouded airport at Newark, New Jersey, lightly dismayed by the urban Northeast. "Is it all like this?" I thought.

I wanted to get to Manhattan's Piccadilly Hotel where I was to rendezvous with other prospective cadets, but I hadn't the slightest idea how to proceed. I found a policeman and told him my problem. He began to talk very rapidly. What language was he speaking? "Excuse me," I interrupted at last. "Would you tell me that again?" He said it again slower, a bit exasperated, I thought. It *was* English, after all. He was from Brooklyn, transplanted to New Jersey.

A bus ride and a fast jaunt in a taxi landed me at the Piccadilly and I joined twenty other scared kids from all parts of the country.

It was nearly eight o'clock when we pulled away from the hotel the next day. The salty old driver threaded the Greyhound bus through the streets of New York and out across the Hudson, then north up the river. The city faded away and trees and hills multiplied.

Burt McCord from Texas sat next to me. We talked in spurts, mostly about how scared we were. There were a few bad jokes and nervous chuckles about getting bounced out of the academy.

Two hours passed, and then unexpectedly we were there. The morning had turned hotter. By ten-thirty, it was hot and muggy; the sun burned down. We passed through the gates and Burt craned his neck to get a better view. I closed my eyes and prayed silently: "Lord, help me not to go out of this gate till I've graduated and made it through. And also, God, if you want me in the ministry, just keep it in my life."

"Drop that bag, Smackhead! Pick it up! Do you hear me? Pick it up, I said! Too slow, Smackhead! Drop it! Pick it up! Too slow! Drop it! Pick it up!"

The senior first classman screamed in my face. I was frozen with fear.

"All right, Smackhead," he yelled even louder, "what's your name?"

I swallowed and began, "My name's Curry Vaughan—"

"What's that? What did you say? From now on, you are to begin with 'Sir, my name is New Cadet Vaughan.' Do you understand?"

There was no time to swallow. "Yes, sir."

"Now," he bellowed, "what's your name?"

"Sir," I blurted, "my name is New Cadet Vaughan."

"Now, Smackhead," the upperclassman growled, "you are going to learn to stand at attention. Do you understand?"

"Yes, sir," I said.

"Louder, Smackhead, louder! I can't hear you!"

"YES, SIR!" I screamed at the top of my voice.

During the next three minutes I was taught to stand at attention with my chin pulled in so hard against my neck that I had to gasp for air. I could barely talk. My body felt as though it

19

were in a straight jacket.

"Now, Dewjerk, that's how you stand every time you go outside your room, whether it's in the halls or at meals. Do you understand?"

I had never seen anyone so vicious. "Yes, sir," I roared.

The entire barracks area was alive with screaming and shouting. The confusion was overwhelming. But it was organized confusion, as time proved, designed to frighten and sober us as we began our lives at West Point. The scene was the Beast Barracks, for new cadets, and it was appropriately named. In a week we would feel we were no longer human, merely beasts. That gang of star athletes, presidents of honor societies, and youth leaders very quickly found they were nothing.

"Now, Mr. Vaughan, you post over to your new orderly room and you report like this, 'Sir, New Cadet Vaughan reports to the first sergeant of the First New Cadet Company for the first time!' " The upperclassman screamed right into my face. His nose was no more than two inches from mine. "Got it? Post!"

I was in a daze, but headed toward my new location, trying desperately to remember what to say. I staggered into the orderly room and mumbled, "Sir, New Cadet—uhh—"

"What's the matter with you, Dumbjohn?" My new tormentor was as loud as the first. "Don't you even know your name?"

"Sir, New Cadet Vaughan reports to the first sergeant of the—First New Cadet—Company—for the first time," I gasped.

In fast order, I was given a haircut, uniforms, and equipment, running back to the first sergeant after each stage and gasping: "Sir, New Cadet Vaughan reports to the first sergeant of the First New Cadet Company for the *second* time," then the "*third* time," and the "*fourth*," and on and on. I had a tag tied to my belt loop that was checked off as we finished each item on the list. I was like a little kid on his first trip to summer camp. By the end of the day, our whole ragtag bunch of shaggy civilians had been trimmed, uniformed, and marched to Trophy Point for swearing-in. I couldn't believe it was really happening to me. Could I cope with it?

Serious tension rose in my personal life right away. It had to be dealt with—and was.

One of the best things to happen to me immediately was to be invited to join a small group of cadets who met every morning for a six-thirty chapel service. They also met in the evenings in scattered parts of the barracks areas for precious minutes of Bible study and prayer in small groups. Sometimes there'd be only two in a group, but they met. And for those few moments, barriers came down. Mighty upperclassmen and lowly plebes were brothers in Christ.

One of those men was Steve, a well-liked first classman. His roommate, while not a Christian, had been impressed by Steve's dedication. I quickly learned how impressed he had been.

It was a late-summer day. Inside the barracks, I charged up a flight of stairs, tripped, and fell hard. Grabbing my throbbing shin, I let loose with a four-letter oath, one that I used altogether too frequently.

Suddenly a gleaming, well-polished pair of shoes stepped into my vision. I stopped, and my eyes rose up over the sharply creased trousers, all the way up to the stiff, high collar of an academy uniform and past the firm chin to the steely eyes of Steve's roommate. I expected icicles to form on his face, his stare was so cold.

With all the fury any upperclassman had hurled at a plebe, he descended upon me. His voice was like the crack of a bullwhip. "Get to attention, you pipsqueak, and stop moaning like a little child. What kind of language is that, Dewjerk? If you think you can talk like that around here, Dumbjohn, you've got a lot to learn, and you don't seem to be learning it very fast. You have a weak head and a filthy mouth. Just who do you think you are?"

And it went on from there—tight-lipped, controlled ferocity and contempt.

He walked away and I continued up the stairs, slowly. I was in shock, not so much from his anger, but from the realization that he knew I was supposed to be the same kind of Christian his roommate was. He had seen me lose control; he had heard me swear. What kind of witness was that? And we had talked a lot in our small groups about our witness. All at once, the facts of my responsibility as a servant of God, as a brother to Steve, and as a declared candidate for the chaplaincy tumbled into place with numbing clarity.

I stood alone in the center of my room and wondered about the kind of life I was leading. I could only conclude that it wasn't a very good one.

I closed my eyes and prayed, still standing. "Lord, I want to give my whole being to you, but I need your help so badly. Just look at my mouth, Lord. It needs cleaning up. Please do it for me. I pledge to try with all my might to bear a good witness for you with my mouth at all times. Help me, please."

In a flash, my mouth was washed clean. I knew it, and time proved it. My prayer was answered; the Lord chastened me, convicted me, and washed my mouth clean all at the same time. It was significant that an alleged man of God had to get his mouth and tongue in order before moving on to other things.

Unhappily, some of the force *behind* the loose mouth and tongue was not dealt with as quickly. The one-sided shootout with Steve's roommate was only the first step.

The Beginning

I was proud of my wrestling skills. At one hundred ninety-five pounds, I was able to seize men fifty pounds heavier and throw them around, moving in and out quickly and often making them look rather clumsy.

That day, my record stood at four victories and one tie. My opponent was not only big, but also brutally strong. As we moved into the third round, the score was tied, but he quickly added a point by staying in control of my movements for more than a minute, scoring what is called "riding time."

Once again we faced each other and moved cautiously around the mat, arms swinging low, looking for a chance to take control. Then just as I lunged, my opponent grabbed my shoulders and quickly wrestled me out of bounds, a legitimate maneuver that forced a break and moved us back into the ring. But then he did it again. He was actually running off the mat, keeping me from scoring. I got angry—mad, furious. Every time I thought I had him, he managed to get a leg out of bounds and break the action. I was stymied, and getting angrier by the second. I was so uptight I rushed into one worthless play after another, ending up with a whistle ordering us to disengage. I was enraged by the calm, confident look on my opponent's face. I was desperate.

I lunged, and he stepped off the mat. Blinded with frustration, I slugged him with my right fist. The referee blew the whistle and looked sternly at me. For the foul, he gave my opponent another point.

Burned up—and showing it—I wrestled the match out, and lost. I did work up enough decency to offer a rather limp handshake and mumble an indecipherable apology, and then headed for the locker room and a shower—still fuming deep down.

Out of nowhere, the coach, an officer, stepped in front of me. He gruffly told me to step into an adjacent room. There, in front of a group of parents, friends, and wrestlers, he gave me a tongue-lashing. He was immaculate, poised, and controlled; I was tired, sweaty, and disgusted.

"That was the worst example of college athletics I've ever seen," he said softly but with iron in his voice. "And it was worse than that—your sportsmanship was nonexistent. You deserve to be reported."

I pulled myself up into what I hoped was a picture of contained fury, looked him in the eye, and said, "All right, sir, if you want to write me up, you just go right ahead and do it!"

I turned my back on him and stalked out. The others in the room were silent, looking from one to the other, then to me, and to the floor.

I yanked open my locker and slumped on the bench in front of it. The senselessness of the last twelve minutes hit like a sledge hammer. I relived every moment of the nine futile minutes of wrestling and the moments of humiliation right afterward. I had been a jerk. And I was in trouble. I suddenly realized the seriousness of my situation. No one ever makes any kind of retort to a superior officer at West Point. I was in for it.

I showered and dressed and was soon once again confronted in the locker room by the coach. His face was like stone. I stood at attention and, as humbly and sincerely as I could, I apologized.

"Sir," I said, "I want to apologize for my unsportsmanlike actions during the wrestling match, sir, and, sir, I also want to apologize for replying to your reprimand—which I really deserved, sir—in a disrespectful manner, sir."

The coach raised his eyebrows. I didn't know what was coming and was scared to death. He looked hard at me and, in a voice calculated to freeze, said softly, "Vaughan, I'm going to throw the book at you. I'm going to hang you as high as I can."

He turned his back on me and walked out.

The rest of the day passed in a blur. I attended the necessary formations, ate the evening meal, and followed the usual routines. I was conscious only of a heavy cloud of gloom hanging right over my head. I was headed for severe disciplinary action.

Preparing mechanically for bed, I heard a soft knock at the door. I responded dully, not really interested in who would be dropping by. But I opened the door, and Joe Caldwell slipped in quietly. I'm not even sure he said anything as he stepped in. Joe was one of the outstanding men at West Point—a star quarterback, a senior, an outstanding student, a popular leader, and a known Christian.

At first, all he said was, "Hello, Curry, how's it going?"

I sat on the edge of the bed, and he did the same. We talked about football, about classes, about home, and about the Lord. It was mostly small talk. But he never mentioned my notorious temper, which he had seen in full display on the practice field, and there was not a word about my bad conduct that day. Everything was encouragement.

"You know, Curry, these are hard days for you—the first couple of years are always hard—but the Lord is with you. He's going to see you through it. He's got your life right in the palm of His hand. All you have to do is really believe that."

I merely stared at the floor.

"And you're not alone, friend," he said after a moment. "You've got a lot of guys supporting you who know just how you feel, and just how hard things are. You've got good brothers in the Lord here."

After two or three seconds of silence, I nodded my head slowly, still staring at the floor, and mumbled, "I know. I know that's true." The perfect example was seated right beside me. Joe had no official obligation to come to my room. He was one of the academy's busiest men. Furthermore, it was getting late, and he faced six A.M. reveille just as I did. But there he sat, and the love of Christ was all over him as he shared my burdens.

Then he began to pray. "Father, Curry and I come to you now in the name of Jesus and we just want to thank you and praise you for taking care of us here. We thank you that you're with us all the time, in everything, that you haven't left us here alone—"

He asked the Lord to govern the difficult days ahead—the closest he came to mentioning my specific problem. And right there in that barracks room, in the midst of the cold, hard-nosed United States Military Academy, the Lord lifted the cloud of gloom that had hung over me for several hours and I was able to smile for the first time.

"Thank you, Lord," I said as Joe concluded his prayer, and I raised my eyes to meet his. "And thank you, Joe. I needed it. But everything's going to be all right."

As Joe closed the door behind him, I knew I had something crucial to do. I eased down onto my knees and placed my elbows on the bed, my chin cupped in my hands, just as I had when I was a little kid. "Lord Jesus," I began softly, "I've got a real problem that I desperately need your help with. It's my temper, Lord—my temper and my insistence on looking good in front of everybody, Lord Jesus. I worry too much about what people think of me, and I'm tired of that. So, right now, Lord, I want to hand all that over to you, and I ask you to take away my temper and my concern about my image. I want to be rid of all this anger and this defensiveness. I want to be like you, Lord. Please forgive me for all the times I've lost my temper, and especially for today. I give this whole aspect of my life over to you."

I turned out the light and climbed into bed. Sleep came quickly.

Discipline at West Point can be carried out at several levels. The highest is administered by the Commandant's Board. An appearance before it usually results in severe punishment—sometimes dismissal from the academy. It was to the Commandant's Board that I received a summons the following Monday.

I stood before the five officers in the stark, white-painted room. The lights seemed very bright. I was deeply concerned that I would be dismissed and I was nervous, but I wasn't afraid.

"Cadet Vaughan," the senior officer said, unsmiling, "you've heard the complaint against you. Please state your case to the board."

I said simply that I had lost my head in the wrestling match, and I made no attempt to justify my poor sportsmanship or my conduct before the coach. The board's decision came quickly. The officers sympathized with my situation and appreciated my forthrightness—my mind raced ahead to try to guess what was coming—but I had damaged the officer-cadet relationship, and that could not be overlooked. The punishment: one month of confinement to my room during free time and twenty-two hours of "walking the Area."

I did everything to maintain my composure in front of the board, but my relief was great. I knew the punishment would not be easy, but I had not been dismissed. "Thank you, Lord," I said under my breath.

The Area is a rectangular concrete courtyard, surrounded by cadet barracks, with a four-faced clock mounted on a tall iron pole at dead center. Its main function is disciplinary. It is there that men assigned to walking duty must walk. In a corps of cadets numbering twenty-two hundred, there were always more than fifty cadets out there during every free hour.

And so I walked—and walked—for a month. At first glance, it looked easy. But I couldn't choose the marching times; I walked when others were enjoying the little free time we got. And weather made no difference; neither did fatigue.

As I walked off a lifetime of hostility, I often recalled Joe's late-night visit and understood something of what God was doing to me, or letting happen to me. Each of those hours of walking was an hour of facing myself, of looking at that lifelong temper and watching it fade. "I have to let it fade right out of my life," I thought as I marched. "I can no longer fly off the handle. I received self-control, a sound mind, when I received Jesus, and I'll have to utilize it."

It was late in the day. I could feel the sweat in the small of my back. My right heel was rubbed raw inside my shoe, and my stomach was absolutely hollow. I tried to keep my eyes straight ahead; we weren't allowed to talk or even look at the other cadets. There were fifty-two of us that day, seemingly milling around in the relatively small area, yet we were orderly if you watched us long enough, performing a strange ballet to an unheard drum.

Suddenly, peace swept over my body like a cool breeze. Suddenly, my foot didn't hurt, and the sweat slipped into insignificance. Suddenly, I wasn't hungry. For probably thirty seconds, I had a glimpse, sort of an incomplete drawing, yet in bright colors, of God working in a man's life—in my life. I started off wobbling and limping as I walked, and I looked fat and sweaty. Before long the wobbling diminished and, somehow, I seemed trimmer and trimmer, and pretty soon I was walking easily, and I looked good. I wasn't wobbling or limping. I was a whole man doing a job. I was mature. Abruptly the vision ended.

Wow! It was a painful process, but God was bringing wholeness into my life. I kept my eyes straight ahead, and my step didn't slacken but, inside, I was awash with joy. "That's what hope is all about," I thought. "Thank you, Father."

As with so much of society at large, awareness of the Lord seems to ebb and flow at West Point. A string of Christianity runs all the way through the academy's history, of course, but often it was a thin string, as with history in general. Times of renewal seem to run in cycles, inside or outside the military. One significant time came at West Point in the fifties. It was a period of strong movement by the Holy Spirit and included ministry by Jack Wyrtzen and other Christian youth leaders, as well as the Officers' Christian Fellowship. It is impossible to tally numbers, but certainly dozens of young men who were preparing for lives of leadership in the United States military, probably hundreds, at one time or another during that period committed their lives to Jesus Christ.

One of the enigmas of that time, also, was the fact that large numbers of the Christians were in the Class of 1951, which was bound for tragedy. That was the class committed into combat in the Korean War without full training. Those young officers were sent directly into action and many died. It was one of several great disasters of that ugly war.

But out of that period came one man who was to shape much of my life and work—King Coffman, a captain at that time, and a graduate of the Class of '52. He was a professor of chemistry, but much more importantly, he was a man of God.

One day he invited Paul Stanley and me out to his home, picking us up in his dilapidated old car. Paul was another football player and follower of Jesus. We didn't know what to expect.

Captain Coffman opened the door and turned to let us pass in front of him. An easy warmth rose in his face. "Come in, fellows, I'm awfully glad you're here." His voice had a strange quality—enthusiastic and soft at the same time. I knew he was glad for us to be there.

We followed him into the brightly lighted living room. He

was a lot taller than I'd realized—tall, slender, and every inch an officer. I still wasn't sure what to expect. All he'd said was to bring our Bibles and we'd talk a bit about the Lord. His wife, a slender, blonde woman, rose from her chair and extended her hand to each of us. I knew instantly that she, too, was glad for us to be there. "I'm Irene Coffman," she said. Her voice was even softer than his; her eyes were soft, too, but shining. She was very pretty. Paul and I looked at one another, smiled, and sat down on the sofa.

"We've been looking at First Thessalonians," Captain Coffman said, picking up a Bible from the table beside him.

That night set in motion more than three years of the closest fellowship I'd known. It was the first step in the Lord's program to remove the negatives from my character and replace them with His Word, at last establishing a foundation for my Christian life. It had been badly needed.

From the two of us, Paul and myself, grew a closely woven group of thirteen cadets sincerely committed to following Jesus Christ above all else. The move of the Holy Spirit was not quite as widespread as that of the fifties, but it was strong and rich, definitely another ring in the cycle of God's activity at West Point.

King Coffman took a personal interest in all of us, constantly, relentlessly encouraging us. He and his wife kept the doors of their quarters open to us, and we spent a lot of time there, collectively and singly. There were group discussions, study sessions, personal counseling. Steadily we were schooled in Bible doctrine and Christian ethics. Steadily we were instilled with Christ's call for discipline in the lives of His followers.

Added to this were our little cell-group Bible studies that each member of the Coffman group held in his own company area every night. Although a cadet's life is rigidly scheduled, some of that prescribed time is listed as "free." One of those free periods was from nine to nine-thirty every weeknight. We took advantage of that time to gather a few cadets in some corner of the barracks and teach them about the Savior. Often there would be only one cadet besides the leader, but we constantly kept before us the words of Matthew 18:20: "For where two or three are gathered together in my name, there am I in the midst of them."

Those were magnificent years of learning, and the Lord used them gently to reach into every corner of the United States Military Academy at some time. Today, one of that group is the president of a small Bible college; several others are in a person-to-person, evangelical ministry called the Navigators, which reaches around the world. Some are still in the military service, line officers with promising careers, living witnesses for Christ in unusual spheres of activity.

Pat Stevens was a star man. The gold stars on either side of the gray, high-collared West Point uniform told the world that Pat was in the top five per cent of his class. He was destined to be a crack officer, a financial wizard, and an enormously likeable human being. His father was stationed at the same post as mine, and when our plebe year finally ended, we headed home together to Fort Monroe, Virginia.

Two days after our arrival, I walked into the Stevens' quarters, and my life took a sharp turn. He introduced me to a young woman with the most beautiful hair I had ever seen. I gawked—stunned, silent, embarrassed. Her beautiful dark hair framed a delicate, oval face, altogether lovely.

"Nancy," Pat said, "this is Curry, the one I wrote you about. Curry, this is my sister."

I couldn't believe it. I'd seen Pat's sister once or twice before, but suddenly it was different.

"Hello, Curry." It was the sweet, cultured voice of so many Southern girls, but the sparkling brown eyes and firm confident chin didn't match the lazy drawl. "She's no ordinary Southern belle," I thought. I still hadn't said anything aloud. She said something and laughed. I wasn't sure what she had said. I looked at Pat, and right back into her quick eyes. Her laugh was so free, but not giggly or silly. She was amused and she laughed, freely. Why couldn't I concentrate better?

My first date with Nancy, the next day, was at the officers' beach club. The sun was magnificent, and the swimming excellent. That night we baby-sat my little sister, Clara, while my parents went bowling. We sat on the sofa, and our conversation began to warm up. There are many things a boy tells a girl—especially a boy of nineteen sitting close on a sofa with the most beautiful girl he has ever met. But somehow I got going down the road of Jesus Christ. I found everything just spilling out of me. "You know, He lives within me now. When I accepted Him as my Lord and Savior, He actually came into my life and lives within me—" I rambled on. "He's been working out a lot of the kinks in my character. He does that, you know, sometimes instantly, sometimes over a period of time. I had problems about cussing, and anger, and ambition—" She seemed to be listening intently, and I plowed on. "He's giving me a purpose for life beyond myself. He's setting a whole bunch of priorities in my life, and I'm just starting to get a handle on them—"

I stopped, and there was silence. It wasn't a cold silence; it was comfortable and quiet. "What it boils down to, Nancy, is that I've put Christ first in my life, and I want Him always to be first—ahead of my career, ahead of my wife and family."

Her eyes lowered ever so slightly. She was very still—"and very pretty," I thought. The only sound was the low hum of the air conditioner. "Have I blown it?" I thought. "I don't want to blow it, Lord."

After fifteen seconds, she looked up. Just the tiniest trace of a smile was on her pretty red lips. But she said nothing.

"What about you, Nancy?" I asked at last. "Do you feel the same way about Christ? Do you know Him?" I gulped. I was sure I had gone too far.

She merely shook her head from one side to the other. Her lips formed the word "no," but they remained silent.

"Well, would you like to try?"

At last, she spoke. "Yes." Her voice was just above a whisper.

I took a deep breath and pushed on, "All you have to do is bow your head, confess that you're in need of a Savior"—how hard it was for me to think of this lovely girl as a sinner—"and ask Jesus to come into your heart."

She prayed almost the exact words I had said but added a few surprising thoughts about how much she needed God to direct her life and how unsure she was in everything. "I want to be yours, Lord," she concluded. Tears spilled all over my face.

She looked up and smiled at me, a radiant smile. "Something happened," she said. "I really feel close to God."

I was thoroughly shaken. That was not my usual line with a beautiful girl, but something unmistakably holy had taken place between us. Someone else had been in control.

I crawled into the spare bed in my parents' quarters that night and realized two things had happened to me that would change the course of my life. I had led someone to Jesus Christ. And I had fallen hopelessly and irrevocably in love.

The next three weeks sped by—wonderful days with Nancy, days of typical teenage romance, but days of togetherness in an atypical dimension. I kissed her goodbye at the airport.

Nancy enrolled that fall in a junior college in Washington, D.C., and came to see me at West Point as often as she could. We were persistent, and that was necessary. Courtship on academy terms is a unique experience. In the day of coed dorms and total student freedom in morals and schedules in most of society, West Point had not shifted more than an inch.

It still observed traditions regarding courtship and dating that hadn't changed in fifty years. Dating was allowed, in fact encouraged. But the cadet was given only a few weekend hours to see his girl. Some weekends began on Friday afternoon at three, but more often they began after a Saturday morning of classes and parades. Always the magic hour was six P.M. on Sunday. And barring a special privilege, the weekend had to be spent on post. When I was playing football, Nancy and I had less than twenty-four hours together.

The girls—some of them uninvited but optimistic, most of them invited guests of cadets—began to arrive at noon on Friday. The lucky ones claimed the reservations made for them by thoughtful cadets at nearby rooming houses or at the tradition-honored Thayer Hotel on post. And the girls almost always paid their own way. Nancy got by on two dollars a night. The accommodations, even at the Thayer, were only vaguely deluxe. Six girls to a room was not exceptional.

"This is as private as we're going to get," I said to Nancy that crisp winter night at the edge of Chesapeake Bay near Fort Monroe. It was Christmas vacation. "And I have some things I'd like to talk about."

She knew what they were. Even in those few hours we'd shared over the last six months, we'd talked frankly and precisely.

"I believe the Lord has called us to live our lives together," I went on matter-of-factly. My breath made little clouds in the cold air. "I'd like to marry you when I graduate. We love each other, and there's no sense waiting."

Her eyes and mouth showed no opposition, so I went on. "And if the Lord has called us together, we ought to act on it. Will you marry me?"

It was as casual as that. "Yes," she said. "I want to marry you.

And I believe God wants me to marry you."

Data suggest that West Point marriages have little more than a fifty per cent chance of success. Interpreters of this divorce rate blame it on the superficial glamor of academy social life and the pressures, separations, and temptations of life in the career of a young officer.

I spoke solemnly to Nancy about this. "It's all the fault of the human condition, however. We're a fallen people. But when we have Christ, we overcome this. And I believe we can make it together."

She nodded.

Fortunately, we had many months ahead with King Coffman and the fellowship at his home. Many couples spent many evenings there, learning and growing. Lasting friendships formed in that living room. I know of several marriages that are on solid ground because they were established in Christ within that little fellowship. And those are lives that touch many parts of the military.

I looked at my watch. Ninety minutes had passed since graduation. There were Nancy's parents, just in from Okinawa. There were my parents. All the faces in the little post chapel were beaming. My grin was stretching the corners of my mouth tight.

I turned, and looked up the aisle. There came Nancy. Her white Chinese brocade dress was exquisite; her beautiful, dark hair was piled high on her head. Suddenly I thought I might collapse. I held on, but as I turned—I was supposed to do only a quarter-turn and stop, but I kept on turning—I was thrown into a daze by the beauty and the wonder. My whole face broke into an uncontrollable, and undoubtedly very foolish-looking, grin. My friends, especially the men, had all they could do to keep from laughing out loud.

As she reached the altar, I could see that her face was wet with quiet tears. The Lord had given her a deep love.

Clumsily, but happily, I slipped the wedding band in place on her delicate finger. It bore an inscription: "United in Christ as one, West Point Chapel, 5 June 1963."

3

DECISION

Life was beautiful. Nancy and I got along so wonderfully well that those days could almost have been the conclusion to a fairy tale. We had been told that after the honeymoon our relationship would change. "Just wait!" came the good-natured but direct warnings. The ominous forecasts of fighting and arguing never came to pass in those star-filled days. We were in love, and together we shared Another's love.

Fort Benning, Georgia, was our first post. There I had to go through the proving ground of infantry, airborne, and ranger courses. And it was a proving ground for new brides, too—a time of adjustment to second place in their husbands' lives at least during that rigorous period, a time of adjustment to the frequent superficiality of social life in the army, a time of loneliness in the midst of activity. And Nancy showed herself as competent in her role of army wife as I did in my role of soldier.

From there, we joined the "Big Red One," the First Infantry Division, at Fort Riley, Kansas, a hot, sprawling installation near the center of our country, where new, life-changing decisions lay.

At first, I was an infantry platoon leader and later moved up to company executive officer. I loved every minute of it. The work was demanding and challenging—leading and dealing with men from every background conceivable on a personal, life-and-death level. But those stimulating challenges were being complicated by the debate rolling back and forth within me over whether I should stay in the infantry. Deep inside I could feel a continual, gentle tug calling me into the full-time ministry as a chaplain. Many years had passed since that soft tug had begun. It had weakened often, but had never vanished since that first moment in my high school freshman year. It was there, like a whisper. But I still had trouble picturing myself as a minister. I was a good soldier, as rough and tough as any, and I liked the infantry. I obviously had a good soldiering career ahead of me if I pressed on. But could God have any purpose for a soldier? Could the Prince of Peace want professional soldiers in His army of faith? And what about the unending whisper?

It was the Christmas season of 1964; a year and a half had passed. Nancy was getting ready for bed, and I was alone in the living room. The whisper was almost a voice that night. "What about your decision to become a chaplain, Curry?" There it was. "You had wanted to serve me with all your being. You had wanted to minister the truth to others." I had never felt thoughts more clearly. They were sharp within my mind.

"Dear Lord," I said under my breath, "you know I've always had this desire to serve you as a chaplain, even from my boyhood days. It's never really gone away, but I'm just afraid of my own weaknesses and my inadequacies. I'm not a smooth, graceful man, Lord, the way so many of your ministers are. . . ."

A flashing thought cut my prayer short. "I will make you smooth." It was just that simple. I instantly knew that God would use my weaknesses and inadequacies, and in fact would turn those to strengths. I instantly knew that all the things that had happened to me, the molding of my character and personality, had been directed by Him. He had been preparing me for the steps He had chosen for me. And, for that moment at least, I sensed this included preparing for the ministry. But still I hedged, "Lord, if you don't want me to go to seminary, close the door. But this is what I feel you are leading me to do."

With that, I submitted the paperwork that would allow me to go to seminary. By God's grace, the chief of chaplains was able to set up an excess-leave program under which I would be permitted to stay in the army while in seminary, but I would not get any pay during that time. Normally, one had to resign from the army to go to seminary, losing significant longevity. It seemed that everything was in motion—for the moment.

Just one week before the day my orders called for us to leave Fort Riley for Columbia Seminary in Decatur, Georgia, my prayer for the Lord to "close the door" if He wanted to slammed right back into my face. I was in the field with my company for a training test. The early evening was hot and dry as summer pressed down upon us.

A jeep pulled up, sending puffs of dust into the air. It was the battalion commander, Colonel Salisbury, a strong, good-looking combat veteran who had become a good friend. He climbed out of his jeep and called me off to one side. "Curry." His voice was hushed. I didn't know what to expect. "This is top secret. It looks like we're going to Southeast Asia. We don't know that for sure, but we have been told we are going to move out to the Pacific. I'm telling you this because it may affect you and cancel your orders to go to seminary."

My stomach pulled tight, and I could feel my heartbeat increasing. I started to breathe heavily, but said nothing. He was watching me closely. "Do you want to stay with the unit?"

All the hard days with all those men swept across my mind.

The loyalties that had been built the hard way, the learning that had come through sweat and anguish, all those relationships, the strenuous fun, my capabilities—they all flashed across my inner eyes.

The colonel continued to stare into my face. I had to say something. "Let me think about it tonight." The sentence was blurted out, wrapped in frustration and desperation. "I'll tell you in the morning."

I stood alone for several minutes. Did I want to stay with the unit? What a question! I had trained and worked with the men of B Company for more than a year and a half. I knew them. It was not sentimentality to say I loved them. I knew the seriousness of the mission—many would die if the "Big Red One" did indeed go to Vietnam. "Lord, help me," I said as I returned to my post.

The field exercise kept me on the radios all night. We didn't go to bed. But every couple of hours came a minute or two of quiet, and I'd get a break. We were situated on the side of a little hill and at every opportunity throughout the night, I walked over the top, just out of sight, and dropped to my knees. I said the same thing each time. "Lord, show me; what am I supposed to do? This is the most difficult decision of my life. I have to know. I have to tell the battalion commander tomorrow."

All night I plodded up and down that hill, hoping for a message from heaven or an angel on a cloud or even a brick on my hard head, but nothing came. Nothing. Up and down. And nothing. The hot Kansas night was silent.

It was nearly ten o'clock and the exercise was critiqued when the battalion commander approached me. He waited until he was right up next to me. "Well, Curry, what did you decide?"

I'd worked up a little answer that was really no answer—a stall—but as I opened my mouth, different words came out. "I'm going to let the powers-that-be decide." I could hardly believe the words had come from me.

The colonel said simply, "Okay." To him those powers were the army and those in governmental authority. But even as I'd spoken, I knew who the real powers-that-be were—Father, Son, and Holy Ghost. Quite surprisingly, I had managed to throw myself entirely upon God. He would decide. I honestly didn't care which way He took me.

As the commander walked away, there was nothing left for me to say except, "Thank you, Lord."

The week passed very slowly. I couldn't say much to Nancy because the information given to me was top secret. I couldn't say anything with certainty to anyone, not even the landlord. The adjutant hadn't given us final approval to move, yet the movers were scheduled to come to get us ready for Decatur.

Finally, it was one day before we were to move, if we were going to seminary. There was a knock at the door. I opened it, and it was the adjutant. "As far as we know," he said, "your orders have not been changed, so you'd better go ahead and move."

We had everything already packed, so out we moved the next morning. That night we stayed with our company commander and his wife. During the evening, the battalion commander called, and I could hear pieces of my host's remarks—enough to determine that the call was about me. My stomach tightened. What now?

My commander walked serious-faced back into the room. "Curry, the boss wants to see you in the morning. That's all I know."

I slept little that night. Nancy had figured out enough to keep her awake, too. She knew it was big decision time.

I walked into the battalion commander's office and saluted. I was tense. He went straight to the point. "Curry, you've been cleared to stay with your unit. But it's up to you." He watched me closely. "What do you want to do now?"

Suddenly, everything was clear, and I spoke without hesitation. "Sir, a day ago, I'd probably have said I'd like to go with the unit, but now I'm on my way to seminary. My furniture is en route to Decatur, and we've said our goodbyes. I think we should go."

He, too, spoke without hesitation. "Fine. That's good. Go."

He came around from behind his desk and we moved toward the door. "It's interesting," he said. "The reason we couldn't get a clearance on you earlier was that your records were floating around in channels between the infantry and adjutant general branches in the Message Center. They just couldn't find your records to get the approval for you to stay and to rescind the earlier orders."

It took several minutes for what he'd said to sink in. Had my records been found one day earlier, or had I planned on one day less travel time, or had any of the other one-day possibilities occurred, my clearance would have come and I quite likely would have agreed to go to the Pacific with my company. As it was, the matter was governed for me. I had only to go through the open door. Some might have said the Lord sneaked me through a crack, but He was the one who managed it.

The days at Columbia passed quickly. I was thrust right into the middle of Greek and Hebrew, into systematic theology, into church history, and my apprehensions soon melted. I was too busy to be apprehensive, trying to keep my head above water in that first intensive summer course.

I was poring over my Greek book one afternoon while Nancy was at work. The air conditioner droned softly and the radio played just loudly enough for me to hear it. Six days a week, two sessions a day, I wrestled with Greek. It seemed to take all my energy. The radio announcer's voice suddenly broke my concentration. It was crisp, clear, and impersonal. "Casualties continue to mount in Vietnam. Among the latest is an area man, Lieutenant Leon Holton."

I gasped and slumped back in my chair. "Leon." I heard myself say the name. "Killed?" I couldn't believe it. He had been my comrade in arms for a year—executive officer of A Company at Fort Riley while I was exec of B Company. He had taken his unit into combat in Vietnam; I had gone to seminary.

I jumped to my feet and lunged at the radio, snapping it off. "God!" I cried aloud. "What am I doing here? I ought to be over there fighting this war with my men and my friends. I don't belong here!" It was stupid and absurd. The son of an army colonel, married to a colonel's daughter, a graduate of West Point—a regular-army, gung-ho, airborne, ranger-qualified infantry officer. Doing what? Listening to war broadcasts in safe Decatur, Georgia, in air-conditioned comfort, studying Greek! And one of the finest soldiers I'd known had been killed.

I was suddenly out of place in a hostile environment. My mind raced wildly. The lexicons and notebooks were alien, worthless objects. I swept them onto the floor and closed my eyes to shut out that hostile environment. My thoughts wandered. I saw the greenness of Vietnam's jungles. I saw my men. I wanted to be with them.

"But you're not there." The thought was like a voice; it was soft and even. "You're here. I led you here."

I opened my eyes. Had there been a voice? I seemed alone. "Yes, Lord," I said. "I'm here. But I need reassurance. Am I in the right place?"

I sat quietly for several moments. It may have been three minutes. Not a sound penetrated the room. I reached for my Bible; maybe reassurance was there. I opened it and read the first thing my eyes came to: "And Jesus said unto him, No man, having put his hand to the plough, and looking back, is fit for the kingdom of God" (Luke 9:62).

My head dropped forward, my eyes closed, and I slipped to my knees. The silence was powerful. God had spoken, and I was awestruck. I finally managed to utter two words. "Yes, Lord."

That night I realized what God had shown me. A good ploughman could not cut straight furrows while looking back. Furthermore, the Lord did not walk behind us, but in front; and our eyes had to be fixed on Him. I had put my hand to the plough and could not look back, even though my soldier's heart yearned to be with my comrades-in-arms.

God was faithful to meet every financial need, even after our firstborn, Virginia, came during the second year. Nancy worked the first year, but the moment she learned she was pregnant, she stopped. I had never known a woman more eager to give her full time to homemaking. She had waited long enough! Meanwhile, I preached in a little country church and we somehow made it, seemingly with plenty to spare. At the end of the second year, the G.I. Bill took over, and our money problems were solved.

It was during this time that I heard people talking about something called the "baptism with the Holy Spirit." I didn't know what they meant. It turned out that some of the people on campus did such things as speak in tongues and meet weekly for what they called prayer and praise meetings. I wasn't impressed. I looked at them and concluded I was a better witness than most of them and as good a student or better. I tallied it up, and I came out on top in every category. Nonetheless, the talk didn't go away. It persisted so long, in fact, that I finally mentioned it to the Lord. "Father, if this experience is a reality—if it is from you—then I want it."

Furthermore, someone gave me a copy of David Wilkerson's book, *The Cross and the Switchblade*, and I read it. It was fascinating, but the chapter on the baptism with the Holy Spirit didn't make much of an impression.

And then a professor from Scotland told one of our theology classes that speaking in tongues was a genuine biblical experience and was for today. "But," he said, "don't try to give it to me." That puzzled me. He thought it was real but didn't want it?

A short time later, a Billy Graham team evangelist spoke at a chapel service. "We have something to learn from the Pentecostals," he said. And those Pentecostals were always talking about the baptism with the Holy Spirit.

Shortly after graduation, a young woman stayed with us during a missionary conference. No matter what I threw against her, she spoke convincingly about the "gifts" of the Holy Spirit. My arguments were outrageous, but she stuck to her guns. Her persistence caused me to wonder.

One incident—one statement—after another. They just didn't stop. I felt I had it all. I was very happy with my relationshp with Jesus. But, just suppose—

I was graduated from seminary on June 3, 1968, ordained to the Presbyterian ministry on June 5, and presented with a second daughter, Julie, on June 7. Nancy witnessed the first two events because the third, Julie's arrival, was delayed three weeks. God's timing was perfect. He gave us five magnificent days.

Three weeks later, we jammed ourselves and our boxer dog, Buck, into the family Volkswagen and headed for my first assignment as a chaplain in the United States Army—Fort Benning, Georgia, which had been our first place of duty after

West Point and marriage.

I was struck nearly dumb as I stood in front of my specific place of assignment—Harmony Church Chapel No. 2. It was at the edge of nowhere. I couldn't believe it. Fort Benning sprawled endlessly, and Harmony Church was at the jumping off place into nothingness. It was as remote as could possibly be, serving the 43rd Engineer Battalion. My words to the post chaplain two hours earlier rang in my ears: "The Harmony Church assignment is fine. I'm willing to serve the Lord anywhere!"

Early the next morning, I headed out to visit my troops. I drove for half a day over rough, bumpy roads to visit a platoon in the field and found only two men asleep in the back of a truck. But I pressed on, grabbing people anywhere I could and inviting them to chapel next Sunday. I repeated the mission the next day, and the next. Frankly, most of the men seemed apathetic, but by the end of the week I was sure we'd have a good service on Sunday.

With the dawning of the radiant Sunday sun, I was exuberant as I reflected on the two-hundred-fifty-seat chapel. My heart was filled with songs and bursts of laughter as I donned my robe and stole. And I opened the door of my tiny office and strode into the sanctuary. Seated in the very last row were four people, including Nancy. That was my congregation. I thought for two seconds that the best thing to do was return to my office and cancel the service. "Lord God, I went to West Point and seminary for *this*? Can it be?"

But I walked to the pulpit and determined to go ahead as though five thousand people were there. To make matters worse, there was no organist. So I blared out three hymn solos—I'm quite certain nothing was coming out of the mouths of my pathetic little congregation. And I prayed as loudly as my rather loud voice could manage. And I preached. Man, did I preach! On "The Glory of the Church"!

In my office after the service, I felt like weeping. Could I have missed God's will so badly?

The next week, the attendance was the same, and the organist still didn't show up. But at least I got Nancy and the three others to move to the front row. The rest was the same. I sang. I prayed. I preached. My voice was the only one heard. I felt like Elijah under the juniper tree, convinced that I was the only one who cared anything about Jesus. But later, alone, I prayed as I'd never prayed in my life. I prayed the prayer of John Knox, with a variation. "God, give me the 43rd Engineer Battalion or I die!" I virtually shouted it.

My old academy buddy and football pal, Paul Stanley, handed me the book. "Let me know what you think of it. I don't want to say anything further."

I turned the paperback over in my hand, as though I might read right through the covers. It was entitled *They Speak With Other Tongues* and was by John Sherrill. I'd never heard of him, but I'd heard plenty about the subject. If Paul said read it, I'd read it.

That night I read it in one sitting, with a kind of open-minded fascination. I put the book down, and my thoughts rambled. I was a committed Christian. I knew the supernatural must be a reality, for Jesus had spoken often about the spiritual world. In fact, I preached that the conversion experience was a supernatural, life-changing transformation. But this book described something that was happening in the denominations of the Christian church right then that was supernatural in new ways. The lives of individuals were full of miracles and spectacular healings. The people were speaking in beautiful languages they didn't know. They were living transformed lives.

At that moment, one part of the book spoke to me directly.

Just the week before, I had labored over Romans 8:26-27 as the text for my sermon:

> Likewise the Spirit also helpeth our infirmities: for we know not what we should pray for as we ought: but the Spirit itself maketh intercession for us with groanings which cannot be uttered.
>
> And he that searcheth the hearts knoweth what is the mind of the Spirit, because he maketh intercession for the saints according to the will of God.

God had blessed me in my labor, but I had approached the text entirely from the traditional and orthodox position. Certainly there was nothing wrong with that approach. It presented the truth. God's Spirit did, in fact, help us to pray. What I had never considered was that Paul might have also been talking about speaking in tongues when he wrote those words. But in Sherrill's book, an individual cited his experience of praying for someone in the hospital in "groanings and sighs too deep for words"! He related that to Romans 8:26-27.

I picked the book back up, and my thumb riffled the pages. The light of the lamp reached out toward the dark corners of the room; the night was still. I strained to grasp the individual's experience. "He surely didn't make it up," I said, just barely audibly.

I was tired. The week had been long, and my hard work seemed to bear so little fruit. I exhaled fully, and took a deep breath. I could feel tears in my eyes. "Oh, God!" I felt myself slipping to the floor. My knees touched. "If there's anything to this, and there's anything more than what you've already given me, I want it." I wept so deeply that my shoulders shook. Had I been stubborn? Stiff-necked?

I handed the book to Paul the next day. "I have to say, old friend, that it moved me. I just don't know what to make of it all."

"You have to admit that the scriptural evidence he uses seems solid," Paul replied.

"Yes, I know." I nodded vigorously. "But I'm just not able to take the whole book."

"I agree," Paul said.

Neither of us had the nerve to voice it, but the prospect of speaking in tongues was frightening for us.

"Besides," I said, "I believe we received the Holy Spirit when we were converted, and there's no more to receive."

Paul didn't say anything, but I felt he agreed with me.

"No more at all," I said conclusively.

Four days later, I walked into the officers' club. It was time for the chaplains' weekly prayer breakfast. After eating, we prayed for several minutes. Men called upon God for renewal, a movement of the Holy Spirit upon the military. It was a powerful time, and I was convinced the Lord was hearing us.

As the post chaplain concluded the prayer time, he rose from his chair. "We're going to see a film this morning. It's about an experience that's being talked about a lot these days—the baptism of the Holy Spirit."

"You're kidding," I said to myself, leaning forward and cupping my chin in my hands with my elbows resting on my knees. This should be interesting.

The lights went out. And a chaplain named Bob Crick, who had been sitting across from me, moved to the empty seat at my right to speak briefly with the chaplain at his right. Crick was a friend, but he had no idea of my recent keen interest in the Holy Spirit experience, and I had no idea he was a member of the Church of God, a Pentecostal denomination. I knew him only as a chaplain who preached Christ.

The film was a series of testimonies, men discussing the experience that had been on my mind so heavily for four days. I was moved as those ordinary people spoke, simply and directly.

The lights came back on. I turned to Crick. "Bob, what do you think of this glossolalia?"

He turned to me; a smile flickered on his face and left. "I was baptized in the Holy Spirit many years ago, Curry." His voice was gentle, and he was very relaxed. "I spoke in tongues back then, and I've been speaking in tongues ever since."

I didn't hear all of the other things he said. I felt as though I'd been punched in the stomach. Here was a real live one! I'd been reading and praying and looking everywhere but here. And here was someone right under my nose who'd had the experience and had spoken in tongues.

I hardly noticed the man sitting down to my left. Crick was still talking, although he nodded and smiled to the man—knowingly, I thought. It was a wiry, energetic Methodist chaplain by the name of Merlin Carothers. He was the one who'd brought the film. I finally turned to him when Crick said, "Ask Merlin here; he'll tell you about it."

I was stunned. Carothers, too? These were two of the finest chaplains I'd encountered. They were greatly respected. What in the world was this they were telling me?

"Bob's right, Curry," Carothers said. "I'm just like you. Good seminary, ordained in a major denomination, respected credentials—all that. But I came to that point where I wasn't making it on my own. I needed more of God. And finally I yielded myself enough that I received an immersion from above—"

My mind wavered at that point, and I lost his words for a moment. "*Immersion from above*?" I said it to myself, trying to focus on his words as he continued. "I was *born* from above," I thought. "What's he talking about—*immersion*?"

". . . and as that immersion—that baptism—occurred, I knew the presence of the Holy Spirit in so great a measure that in a few moments I began to praise God in a language that wasn't mine—one that I didn't know. I spoke in unknown tongues."

He smiled. I knew perplexity covered my face. I looked at Bob. He smiled, too.

"And I've been praying that way ever since," Carothers added, practically slapping his knee with the palm of his right hand.

My heart was pounding. They were introducing me to an entirely different, scripturally-based experience, one in which I was thoroughly ignorant despite what had happened during the last few days. I had never felt the way I did at that moment. I wasn't sure I was breathing. These two guys were respected, solid ministers. They wouldn't take me down the wrong path. Would they? My mind was saying, "Maybe, maybe, maybe." But something seemed to be struggling against that fear. I could almost hear it. "It's right, it's right, it's right." My heart pounded. My mind raced. I wanted the Holy Spirit to do for me what he had done for these men, for those who had testified on the screen, for John Sherrill—and for those I'd read so much about in the Book of Acts.

I shrugged my shoulders and looked from one to the other. "Will you pray for me?"

They responded with one voice. "Sure!"

They rose from their chairs. I think Crick was the first up, and I believe it was he who asked something I wasn't expecting: "Are you willing to be a fool for Christ?"

Wham! What did that mean? I was silent for several seconds. "Well, yes," I thought. "I'm willing to be a fool for Christ. I'm willing to be anything for Christ." I nodded my head at last, and spoke softly but clearly, "Yes."

As I turned my head, I saw that the door to the main lobby of the officers' club was open. The thoughts all ran together. I felt it was probably important that I leave my chair, kneel, and receive this mighty supernatural experience in full view of anyone who might happen into the club. But Merlin stepped quietly to the door and closed it. "This wouldn't be considerate of those milling around out there," he said. "The Holy Spirit is a gentleman."

The next thing I knew their hands were on top of my head, and they were praying. I closed my eyes. I waited with some expectation, but frankly not *too* much. Quite spontaneously, I pulled my head all the way back until my face was aimed at the ceiling, and my eyes were still closed. Before I knew it, my arms were raised. I was seeking and reaching out for God. I had never done that before. Again spontaneously, I began to talk aloud. I uttered quite normal, even fluent, sounds, but in a new language. It was not English. It was an incredibly joyful sound, and I felt incredibly joyful inside. I felt pure and sweet, fresh and whole. I had a language of praise! Could that be? Yes! It was true. I was speaking. And, of all things, I recognized some of the words as Hebrew. I had studied the language in seminary, but knew only enough to speak a few words on my own without reading from a Hebrew Bible. But I was speaking at least some words in Hebrew. I could tell by the sound, even though I didn't know everything I was saying. But it had to be praise. I was so full of joy and worship. It had to be praise.

And what a way to praise the Lord! Here was a Presbyterian, with a Methodist on one side and a traditional Pentecostal on the other. We were glorifying God, each in his own special language.

I hugged both chaplains enthusiastically as we rose to leave, something else I'd never done before. I was almost beside myself with joy and excitement, and yet I was perfectly peaceful. I drove back to my office, speaking in tongues all the way. "Look out, soldiers!" I laughed out loud.

4

LESSONS

I burst into my office, filled with joy and power, and walked to the chair behind my desk. I sat down. Then I got back up. I walked out in front of the desk and turned around. Then I walked back and forth in the room. I was happier than I could remember being since my wedding. I began to speak in tongues again. It was beautiful. I was talking to God! And saying all the things that needed saying. It just kept coming, and I tasted new freedom right there.

I knelt in the middle of the office and mingled unknown languages with English, back and forth, as I felt inclined. Then came quietness, softness, gentleness. Over and over came the words: "I love you, Jesus. I love you, Jesus. I love you, Jesus." I had no idea how many times I said it. I was aware only that I loved Him, and knew it deeply. All embarrassment, all tentativeness, slipped quietly away.

The day swept by. I worked on my sermon, wrote the notices for the bulletin, counseled two soldiers, and sat and stared.

"I must tell Nancy." The thought broke into my consciousness. I chuckled aloud. "I've been so caught up in all this, I've forgotten her." We'd shared everything; we mustn't stop now.

I pushed open the door to our little apartment and rushed in. "Nancy! Nancy! I've got it, I've got it!"

Apron neatly in place, she stepped from the kitchen into the room. Her eyes were wide. "What is it, Curry? Got what?"

"I've got the Holy Spirit!" My voice was too loud, and I rushed toward her with my arms wide. "Jesus has baptized me with His Spirit! He really did it!"

Puzzlement flooded her face as my arms enveloped her. "What's that?" she asked, her voice slightly muffled against my shoulder.

She led me into the kitchen and I poured out everything I could remember. It was a torrent. It wasn't long before I had her back in the living room and down on her knees, confessing her sins. I laid my hands on her head and shouted to God. Later reflection brought embarrassment. I really shouted. I was insistent. "Jesus, baptize my wife with your Spirit!" I demanded.

Then I prayed, and I prayed. But nothing happened—except that I frightened Nancy half to death. (Actually, I believe she received the baptism with the Spirit by faith at that time, although she did not speak in tongues or show any other manifestation.)

After supper, I rushed over to the homes of all my close friends and told them what had happened to me. I threw all caution to the wind. I was sure I had such a walk with Jesus at that moment that nothing could stop me—Satan or anyone else.

It wasn't long before I was convinced that I was the John the Baptist of the twentieth century and that I was going to be instrumental in a revival that would ripple from Fort Benning to California and back across to New York. I was frenzied, zealous, desirous of seeing God's work done. I rushed on and on. During prayer one time, I even spoke through my own lips that I would fall, be raised up again, and finally be greatly and powerfully used by the Lord. But I charged on.

People were being won to Christ all around us. Things were even picking up at Harmony Church. There were a few healings; even some demons were cast out. I roared on.

One day a chaplain friend told me of a problem his wife was having. "Why," I announced, "she has a demon in her. I'll come over and we'll pray for her and cast it out."

He gave me a strange look, but said nothing.

Later that day, I took Nancy by the arm and we went to their home, arriving just as they were beginning dinner. They had a guest—a distinguished judge. Unflinching, I charged on in. They had little choice but to invite us to join them.

We made small talk for a while as the room slowly darkened with the sunset. No one had turned on the lights. Suddenly, I figured it was time, and I spoke. "Mrs. ——, the Lord has revealed to me that you have a demon in you. I have come to cast it out in the name of Jesus."

There was absolute silence. No one moved a muscle. For a moment I was scared—"they must think I'm insane," I thought—and I began to feel very foolish. But I was convinced God was leading me, so I went on. "Let's join our hands and pray." We all joined hands around the table and bowed our heads.

"Now, Mrs. ——, please follow me in this prayer: 'Dear Jesus—'" I waited. Silence. "Mrs. ——, please follow me. 'Dear Jesus—'" Total silence.

I rose from my chair, walked around the table to the woman and, standing behind her, laid my hands on her head. "Demon, in the name of Jesus, I rebuke you and cast you into hell!" I shouted with enough power and fury to cast out any demon. Nothing happened. I shouted again. "I come against you in the name of Jesus." The volume was even higher. I felt my face flush with embarrassment, and I stopped. No one knew what to say. I mumbled something about the power of prayer and kept quiet during the few awkward minutes before the table was cleared.

Poor Nancy. While we men went into another room and sat down, she was left to try to carry on a conversation with the woman. As for me, I couldn't figure out what had gone wrong. I was certain I had felt the presence of God with us.

I continued to rush from place to place. My body became weak and tired, and I began to lose weight. Three weeks had passed since my baptism with the Holy Spirit. I assumed I was doing all right—after all, some good things were happening—but actually I felt miserable and knew I couldn't keep going at that rate much longer. "This is sure some crazy pace the Lord has me on," I said to myself.

I was being given verse after verse of Scripture to support my actions. This seemed to keep me blind to my frenzy and confusion. Two friends tried to get me aside for a couple of minutes of talk, but I couldn't pick up what they were saying. I was like a runaway locomotive on the side of a mountain. The throttle was wide open, and someone was throwing coal on as fast as he could.

Three other friends finally collared me one Saturday morning. "Curry," one said, "we've got to talk to you about some very important things, and we're not taking no for an answer."

I knew they were upset about the baptism with the Spirit, and I naturally assumed they just didn't understand. But I agreed to see them that Sunday night at my apartment. "They'll just try to shoot me down," I thought as they walked away, "but I'm ready for them."

I went to my chapel's youth fellowship meeting late that Sunday afternoon, and most unexpectedly—without any solicitation—the Lord began to speak to me. He caused my wild experiences of the last three weeks to pass systematically before my inner eyes, and I saw some definite questions regarding them. They contained no peace. Then I remembered I had been given Scripture verse after Scripture verse to endorse those actions. "Could Satan give those to me?" I mused. "No!" I set my jaw. "Absolutely not. I belong to Jesus."

But I couldn't stop thinking about it. The youth meeting ended, and I headed home to meet with my three friends. But I had a few minutes. "I think I'll go see Merlin about this." So I drove to Carothers' chapel to have a few words with my old friend.

As I walked in, a Moody science film was being shown. The room was quite dark, so I found a chair and sat down. I watched the screen. A blindfolded man seated on a revolving stool was being spun around to the right. He spoke through the microphone mounted on his chest. "I'm going to the right, faster and faster," he said. Then, without anyone telling the man, the stool was stopped, and turned to the left. "I'm slowing down, slower, slower," he said. "Now I'm stopped." In reality, he was going to the left rather rapidly. "Now, I'm going to the left, faster, faster—"

Pilots call this phenomenon vertigo. As the film commentator then explained, "Sometimes we feel we're experiencing one thing when, in reality, something else is happening. That's why we must be careful to discern that God is speaking to us, rather than the enemy."

Zing! I could almost feel the finger pointed at me.

When the group was dismissed, I asked Merlin to go with me to his office for a moment. He shut the door quietly behind him and looked at me. I let two or three seconds of silence pass.

"Merlin, tell me. Can the devil give us verses of Scripture? I know he quoted passages to Jesus, but could he do that to me?"

Carothers watched my eyes closely, pausing. His face was serious. "Yes. I believe he can. Yes."

I exhaled rapidly. Apparently I had been holding my breath. As I did so, I sensed the chains of hell being smashed into a million pieces. In that instant, God set me free and revealed the work of Satan—deception. I had allowed him to deceive me.

Merlin's face was full of kindness, showing no traces of condemnation. He put his hand on my shoulder, and before I knew it was praying. "Lord Jesus, thank you that Satan has no power over us because of you. Thank you that we are free. Now, Lord, keep my brother and me close to you and free from all deception. Your Word promises we'll know your voice and your peace. We expect that to be true in our lives, for we ask it in Jesus' name. Amen."

I dashed out of the chapel into the coolness of the evening with a new release in my soul, although I was disappointed in my conduct—my misguided zeal—over the last three weeks. Satan had actually convinced me I was something I wasn't. My ego was badly bruised. What a fool I had been. But even at that moment, I knew God understood and had forgiven me. He had directly intervened at just the right moment.

At exactly eight o'clock, there was a knock at the front door. It was my three friends. I opened the door, and there they stood, Bibles under their arms, as grim-faced as a vigilante committee.

I asked them to sit down, and took a deep breath. Before anyone could say a word, I spoke. "I want to say a few things, fellows." I spoke slowly at first. "God has just revealed some very important things to me." I could see their hands tense. They glanced sideways at one another, but I went on. "I realize now that Satan has been able to get at me and convince me of some untruths. I also realize that I have been an instrument of deception in his hand. I know that God has done something very real and beautiful in my life—and it can't be denied. The baptism with the Holy Spirit is real. I don't exactly understand it all, but I have now resolved to step back and take a new look at the whole experience. I plan to study God's Word like I never have before, and find out from Him exactly what is of Him and what is not."

Their faces were pale with astonishment. They were thoroughly disarmed, and didn't even open their Bibles.

The next day I was exhausted. The three-week experience had taken its toll. I left my office early and struggled home to bed. I was close to sleep when the doorbell rang, so I staggered down the hallway just as Nancy approached from the other direction. We opened the door together to the wife of an acquaintance of mine. She looked sternly at me. "Boy, I'm glad I believe in eternal security. Because I'm sure you'd be lost forever after all you've done!" She was deeply troubled.

I turned around and went back to bed. I was too tired to explain or to fight back. It was the first of the repercussions we had to ride through from my days of frenzy and confusion. The attacks of the enemy had turned, and now we were being hurt by close friends and neighbors. Most of them turned their backs one by one on Nancy and me. They spoke, but the chill of their words hung in the air. There were no more visits or friendly phone calls.

One brother knocked on the door one night. He sat in my living room and gave me a questioning that was worse than any mounted by a presbytery. Finally, he reached into his pocket and took out a check I had given to his group. He handed it to me.

"What do you mean?" I asked. "I gave that to the Lord for your ministry."

"I don't want it," he said flatly. "I question the motive and everything about it."

I grieved as he left, even though I had managed to refuse the check. I knew then that Christians had great potential to inflict pain. I knew that a Christian had never really been hurt until he had been hurt by another Christian.

In spite of the trials, I fulfilled my promise to my three friends and studied the Bible harder than I ever had. I began to understand things that had always been so puzzling. I began to relax and allow the Spirit to lead me in the study of the Word. I gradually entered into the greatest single benefit of moving into the realm of the Spirit: ever so slowly learning to trust God to lead me in the work of ministry. I learned to wait upon the Lord—not endlessly but until He was ready to reveal His will. I began to learn His voice, my own voice, and Satan's voice.

It was a time of testing. It almost seemed I was back in seminary learning the basic principles of the faith again. And happily I learned that my stumbling entrance into the walk in the Spirit was not unique. It was just that I had not paid any attention to the warnings. Now I knew the warnings had been proper. Any Christian receiving a blessing from God, and especially the baptism of the Spirit, was faced with a "wilderness experience," much as Jesus was shortly after the Holy Spirit had come upon Him at His own baptism with water at the hands of John the Baptist (Matt. 3:16). He was led into the wilderness that He might be tested. That was the pattern. I had moved into the walk in the Spirit, and there had been temptations centered, in my case, on ego, zealousness, and a certain amount of legalism. I had passed through, with God's very direct help, and now there must be no turning back. It was time to move on into the Promised Land and not settle for the small beachhead that had been established. It was time to leave the wilderness once and for all.

The words of Derek Prince, the Bible teacher, became very real to me. "As God gave the children of Israel a promised land," he once said, "He gave us a land of promises. As they had to fight physically to take that land, so do we have to fight spiritually to take what is before us."

I now had to move on off my beachhead and fight for the "land of promises"—but with equilibrium and the strength, the wisdom, the knowledge of the Lord, not on my own. He was teaching me dependence and balance.

Further insight into the problem of testing came in a day or two from Merlin Carothers. He knew the problems I was having. "We have to just praise the Lord for each event, whether it be good or bad," he said. "That's what the Bible says to do in Ephesians 5:20 and also in 1 Thessalonians 5:18."

The words of those verses struck home. I read them when I returned to my office that afternoon. My ingratitude rose before me like a huge boulder blocking my path. I fell flat on my face on the floor. "Oh, God, forgive me. I see it now. I have not acknowledged your right to do with me as you see fit. I have not trusted you in the bad times, but only in the good. I have denied you, Lord. Please forgive me."

Immediately the Spirit brought Peter and the time of his denials of the Lord to my mind. In those moments I relived his experience, and cried out, with tears streaming down my face, "Oh, Lord, thank you for Peter and thank you for all these experiences I'm going through. I've been denying you as I've denied your rights over me. I know now that all this is for a purpose. I thank you."

I was greatly relieved as I drove home in the slanting, late-afternoon sunlight. The rays splashed brightly off the walls of our building as I entered, momentarily blinded as I stepped from the brightness into the hallway darkness. I was immediately met by the wife of a fellow chaplain. She was close to hysteria. "Curry, quick, get to the hospital! Virginia has just swallowed a glass of mineral spirits!"

Without saying a word, I spun and sprinted back into the sunshine, yanking the car door open. I raced toward the hospital. Suddenly, realization struck. Where was the peace, the trust, of fifteen minutes earlier? "Lord, I see this as another test that you're letting Satan put me through, and I'm going to believe in your name that Virginia is all right. I thank you for this experience!"

By the time I drove into the hospital parking lot, I was completely unafraid. The peace was real.

Walking into the emergency room, I saw my little two-year-old daughter, limp and whimpering very weakly as they pumped out her stomach. After several minutes of that gruesome procedure, they lifted her and strapped her into a rig to X-ray her lungs.

After several more minutes I took her frail little body in my arms and held her as the doctor spoke to Nancy and me. "She'll develop a very high degree of fever," he said. "You'll have to expect it and try your best to keep her cool. And it's highly probable she'll develop pneumonia as a result of the inflammation in her lungs."

I looked at Nancy, and back to the doctor, and then at Virginia. I smiled at her, and she smiled back. "Thank you, doctor." We drove home.

Later, I went into the girls' bedroom and once again held Virginia close to me. "Lord," I said in a low voice, but clearly, "I love you. And I have thanked you for this moment. But I rejoice and I thank you in the name of Jesus that Virginia will not get either the fever or the pneumonia."

Nancy and I put her to bed and then went to sleep ourselves.

The next morning, Virginia was up as early as ever, and was as well and happy as I'd ever seen her.

My whole ministry and life style, without any extraordinary effort by me, steadily centered more and more on Jesus and His Word. I prayed and I studied hours at a time each day. That's the only explanation I can give for my progress in the ministry. I had certainly not made myself a popular figure. I had no poise or polish. But the Lord opened the way for me to move ahead. After the humble beginnings at Harmony Church, He saw fit to send me to the main post chapel. I hadn't exactly won the 43rd Engineer Battalion to the Lord, but a strong witness had been made there, and I was given the opportunity for a bigger pulpit. It lasted three weeks.

Then came the word that I would be in South Vietnam in two months. I faced new battlegrounds. I was excited and anxious at the same time; I had many uncertain feelings. My nursery school days were over, and a year of separation and hardship lay just ahead.

I sat in my office as evening began to fall. It was one of the few places where I could be alone. "Lord Jesus." Once again, I was on my knees on the hard floor. "Lord, I'm a soldier. It's the only life I've ever known. Help me to minister the way you want me to. I don't really understand the relationship of soldiers to your plan for the world. And I don't even fully understand my relationship to that plan." I paused. Articulation of my feelings faltered. "Lord, I guess I just want to know what your will is . . . not only for me . . . but for the military . . . and for these wars . . . and for these men I'm going to be trying to help. Show me the way, Lord. What do you want for us?"

The room was quiet. I opened my eyes, and the late afternoon light was very dim. The air seemed tan and brown in the small room. I squeezed my eyes tight.

"Here I am, Lord."

5

THE BATTLEFIELD

The VW van was packed. The last of the furniture had been carried off to storage, and Nancy and I stood in the bare living room. The two girls were playing in the hall. I took Nancy's hands in mine and faced her. "Lord Jesus"—I spoke softly, but the words echoed in the empty room— "we believe we're moving in your will, and we thank you for it. We also thank you for these five months here at Benning. And now we ask you to take us safely to California. Watch over us and take care of us. Please give us good weather and get us to our destination on time. We ask it in your name. Amen."

Those five months at Fort Benning seemed like five years as we looked back. They had given me an experience and a confidence in God that I had never felt. My life was far from perfect, but knowing Jesus through the immersion in His Spirit made me love Him beyond human understanding. This was difficult for me to put into words; I knew only that I loved my Lord with all my might. I knew also that my experience was my own; I could not impose it on anyone else. For every one hundred people who would receive the baptism with the Holy Spirit, there would be one hundred experiences. There might be similarities, but much would be different, for Jesus Christ dealt in individual lives and situations.

We drove north to Indiana and then headed west toward California. It was the middle of January and rough weather was expected, but our prayer was answered. Snow preceded us and followed us, but we chugged along through good weather all the way.

We pulled into the driveway of the home of Nancy's father in Novato, California, in bright, warm weather. It felt good. Nancy would be staying there, and I immediately felt reassured—from several directions.

The next morning, for instance, Nancy's dad and I climbed into the VW and drove several blocks past nicely kept homes and trimmed lawns toward a grocery store. As we were going down the road, I noticed unusual movement in the rear of the van as reflected in the outside mirror. I pulled over, examined the left rear wheel, and found it quite loose. Something was wrong, but I had no idea what. So we returned immediately to the house. There I called a dealer and tried to describe the problem. He suggested I bring it in, but I told him that wouldn't be a good idea; I didn't want anything crucial to fall off while I was driving.

Finally, I decided to go to the dealer in another car and show him what was wrong the best I could. Just before I left, I took another look underneath my van and discovered that a bolt was missing. The hole indicated it was about the size of my little finger. At the dealer's, I took the head mechanic out and showed him on one of his vehicles what was missing.

"Holy mackerel!" he said. "That's the trailing arm bolt."

"What's that?" I asked.

"That, my friend, holds the entire rear assembly of your car together. Right now there's nothing but friction holding your wheel on. You know, yours is the first one of these I've ever seen come off."

"I guess none of the others made it this far." I chuckled, but the mechanic ignored the joke. He went back inside for a new bolt, and I remained squatting beside the van. "Heavenly Father, I thank you for this protection of my family. I thank you for watching over us."

Such reassurance made a man headed for combat feel considerably better.

The pilot's voice came thinly over the speaker. "We're now over Vietnam. We will be landing in fifteen minutes."

I looked out the window. It was hard to believe; the countryside seemed so green and beautiful. Could this be a land of war?

In Long Binh, I spent the rest of the day running in several directions at once, getting processed into the Replacement Detachment. Pushing forward eagerly with all the rest, I eventually learned that I would be joining the 173rd Airborne Brigade at Camp Rock near Bao Loc—a small, dirty, but picturesque village north of Saigon, one of the most beautiful areas in South Vietnam.

Before dawn the next morning I was up and on my way back to the airport. There a hundred of us were crammed into a C-130 cargo plane, sitting on the floor with our knees pulled up to our chests. They called it combat loading. A sweaty, one-hour ride followed, and we were in An Khe. My bags weighed a ton as I stepped carefully from the aircraft right into a hundred-degree blast of air. It was startling.

About the time I was settled into my temporary barracks, I got word I was to go to Bon Song to meet my brigade chaplain. So the next morning I took my first ride in a Huey helicopter, Vietnam-style. The flight was unforgettable, and it was just the first of many. We flew just a few feet off the ground, below the level of most treetops, popping up occasionally to clear a house or village, and then dropping right back down. I prayed in tongues almost the whole time, deeply grateful for the skills of the pilots and the quality of their machines.

My boss greeted me warmly at Bon Song, where I spent the night. I knew he was grateful for any help he could get with what seemed like an impossible task. The next morning, it was right back to An Khe and the airstrip, where I waited with my assistant, Bill, for an airplane to take me to my new home. He had come from Camp Rock to meet me. My eyes kept drifting to him as we leaned against the wall of a small building. He was a fine, clean-cut young man, and seemed sincere enough, but he was covered from head to foot with red dust. I couldn't figure it out.

We waited five hours in the blistering sun, and then spent two more hours on a noisy C-123. Several of the men were airsick, which elevated my natural anxiety considerably.

As I got off the plane, I had my first sobering glimpse of the war. Four men were placing a brown body bag containing a dead man aboard the plane I had arrived in. I stopped for several seconds and watched, wondering how the man had died. My thoughts were filled with heroics. I later learned that he had been one of numerous insane tragedies of the war. He had gotten drunk and wandered beyond the wire outside the compound. As he was coming in, he kicked off a trip flare, immediately screaming, "Don't shoot!" But it was too late. The guards on duty, thinking they were under attack, as they had so often been, had cut him down.

(Camp Rock, by then, was relatively safe. But shortly before I arrived, it had been overrun by the Viet Cong and several Americans had been killed. I immediately was psyched up about that raid—about how the enemy had literally run right through the place, throwing grenades around, and tearing everything up. I figured they could do it again just about anytime they wanted. A couple of days after arrived, I woke up with a start about one o'clock in the morning. I looked out and could see the flashes. I heard the sentry yelling, "Incoming! Incoming!" I grabbed my boots, pulled them on, and then couldn't get them tied. My fingers wouldn't work. A terrible thought flashed through my mind: "You don't know what to do! Hide? Where?" In a second, it was all over. It turned out that it had been our own men throwing grenades out there. I never did know why. But I made a point of finding out right away about procedures under such attack.)

The afternoon was nearly gone as Bill and I arrived that first day. We drove down the dusty road to the compound. Soon he pointed and spoke happily—three months in that hot, exhausting place had not subdued his enthusiasm—"Chaplain, there's our home!"

I followed his finger. It was pointed at a little tent —tired-looking, worn, and situated right in front of the entrance to the compound. Every man and vehicle that went in or out of Camp Rock passed by it. The front and back of the tent were open, and the dirt and red dust blew freely. "So that's why he's covered with red dust!" I chuckled as I winced. After five days, I had made it from the beautiful sunny shores of California to my own private dust bowl.

I counted slowly. Five. My first Sunday service in South Vietnam was attended by five men. The generator outside the briefing tent barked sharply, and I had to keep my voice high to be heard even by the handful there. Distractions were everywhere, but I pushed on to share a few thoughts about Romans 8:28: "And we know that all things work together for good to them that love God, to them who are the called according to his purpose."

"They're all so young," I thought as I watched them carefully. They were all clean shaven, with close-cropped hair.

I thought of my youth group back at Benning.

"That's a piece of Scripture that I believe with all my heart you can hang your hat on," I concluded. "It means just what it says. I've seen it work in my own case. If we really give ourselves to God and let Him run our lives to the greatest extent we can, He will cause all the things that happen in our lives to work out for good. And that includes being in a war."

I led the five in prayer and ended the service. Despite the small beginning, I was filled with an unusual excitement about what the Lord was going to do with the battalion. I cleared away the makeshift altar and talked silently to the Lord about it. "Father, this is your work. Please reach these men for your Son. Stir up their interest in the gospel."

Two days later, I held my first service in the field, with Charlie Company. I arrived in late morning and was greeted warmly by the commander and the first sergeant. "Hello, chaplain," Captain Crowe said. He, like everyone else, seemed young. "Come and join Sergeant Villagomez and me for a bite to eat."

We sat in the clearing and ate C-rations, as plans for a worship service were passed along to the men. About thirty came and joined us. We began by singing; it wasn't much musically, but my scalp tingled as I watched those young guys singing to the glory of God to the best of their ability.

As I had with the five two days earlier, I shared Romans 8:28 with them. "These are things you can stand on, fellows. This is from God's Word, and we've got to let it work all through us so we believe it through the bad as well as the good. God loves us. He's concerned about us. He will take care of us no matter what—even if we die."

We had a good few minutes together. For the first time in those early days I experienced the cameraderie and the good fellowship that I was to know with the men through all kinds of circumstances in the next year. I was happy to be there, and they were happy for me to be there. Nearly all thirty stopped to shake my hand vigorously. "See you next week, chappie," they said over and over.

And that established the pattern. I made a point of being at Camp Rock every Sunday for services. Then on weekdays I visited the four line companies in the field. Depending on how the men were spread around—where the platoons were—I would do five to fourteen services a week. And that was where I found my heart lingering—in the field. There was the loneliness, the fear. There were the poor in spirit. As often as possible I went out into the field to live with the smaller units for a day or two at a time, not merely to conduct services, but to see the men right where they were.

My first such living experience in the field came with Alpha Company. The commander, Captain Wass de Czega, was shrewd and unusually capable, always warm and receptive when I came to be with the men. I was amazed I could actually have fun in that ugly, war-torn situation, but I found that the first time out with A Company was genuine fun because of the men.

I put on my rucksack and set out into the boondocks with them. At first I was unable to get my mind off the ever-present threat of attack by the jungle-wise enemy we knew lurked in and around such sun-darkened places. My awareness of the danger never fully left me, but my ability to function in spite of it improved.

On our third day out came my memorable moment of those first weeks. We had reached our destination by early afternoon and there, on the side of a rolling green hill, I held a service for the entire company. Using a wooden ammunition box, I set up my little altar, with the tiny gold cross and the communion elements, draped my black stole around my neck, and led the men—black, white, city-born, country-born, educated, uneducated—in worship of the Lord. We sang, I spoke from the Bible, and we prayed. I was the only one who spoke audibly, but I saw many lips moving silently in the afternoon sunlight.

As I spoke, my eyes kept landing on one soldier seated in the middle of my dirty, grubby-looking parish. I had met him earlier and knew him only as Bucky. After the service, I shook hands with everyone, and Bucky kept hanging around the edge of the cluster around me. After a while, most had left, but Bucky stayed.

"Where are you from, Bucky?" I asked.

"Near Omaha."

"Did you go to church there?"

"Some." He was quite shy, and looked at his boots a lot as we talked. But he continued to open up.

"Did you ever ask Jesus Christ into your life?"

He looked up quickly into my face. There were several seconds of silence, and he looked at his boots again. "No. I don't think so. No." He spoke slowly. "No, chaplain, I never did."

"Would you like to right now?"

"You mean . . . here . . . now?" He looked into my eyes.

"Sure," I said, smiling. "We can pray right here. Just the two of us."

None of the other men were within earshot. I watched Bucky's face.

"Yes, chaplain, I'd like to."

"Fine." My heart was beating rapidly. I was excited. "Let's just bow our heads."

I waited a moment. I was not aware of any noises except an occasional murmur from some of the men. I heard what sounded like a mess kit clanging some distance away.

"Bucky, my brother, just follow me in prayer. Repeat after me: 'Lord Jesus, I open the door of my life, and I ask you to come in and be my Savior and my Lord. Wash me clean by your blood and forgive me my sins, in your name. Amen.' "

My heart pounded. I took hold of his arm, and gripped it tightly for a moment as he uttered the "amen," softly but conclusively. He meant it. "He's born again," I shouted inside. I wanted to jump up and down and shout it to the world from that soft, green hillside, but I knew Bucky wouldn't be able to handle any embarrassment right at that moment.

"Bucky"—I released my grip on his arm—"you have taken the most important step a man can take. You have been born again. You have stepped into the kingdom of God. Now don't you ever doubt it. Stand on it. You belong to Jesus Christ and to the Father. Don't ever forget it."

He smiled, but said nothing. Finally, he nodded and walked away.

I walked around a bit lightheaded the rest of the day. Bucky was the first person I had led to Christ in my battlefield assignment.

That night, before dropping off to sleep, I thought about Bucky and our special minutes together. I thought about the other men. I thought about those who hated being there, and about those professional soldiers who were doing what they had been assigned to do. I thought about the young company commanders, and the older officers.

"Lord Jesus." I'm sure none of the words were audible in the starry night, but I was very aware of the presence of Christ. "Thank you for letting me see my purpose in being here. Thank you for Bucky. I know I must preach the gospel to every man possible and lead everyone I can to you. I know I'm not here only to console people. Thank you for letting me see that. Please bring all these men to yourself. Please grant them eternal life."

As I stared into the night, my mission before me was bright as day.

"I'm not sure which is worse, these steep mountains or those horrible swamps." I was talking to myself as the sun's rays seemed to pound down on my helmet. I was in good shape, but the going was rough and I breathed harder and harder. My legs just didn't want to take that next step.

But the swamp had been terrible. I couldn't stand the leeches. They were gross looking and their bite was worse. And I knew there were worse things out there, too. The water had reached to my armpits and I was afraid I might stumble, as some of the fellows had. I didn't want to go all the way under. I knew the leeches were all over my legs and body. "Yuck!" I found myself spitting it out audibly. "Hang on, chappie," the sergeant in front of me said. "We're almost through it."

And then came the elephant grass. It made painful slashes in any bare skin it touched—arms, necks, faces. It was razor sharp. The cuts made good feeding for the insects.

During breaks, some of the men wondered aloud about what we were doing there. As with some of the American civilian population, there were serious doubts among some of the men about the correctness of United States involvement in this war. But most of the time, our bodies were working so hard to survive that we didn't dwell on much of anything except getting up the next hill or finding the next stream to replenish our water supply. We were continuously in life-or-death situations and couldn't spend much time debating the political aspects of the war.

We were in the hills when we ran out of water. The trip had been bad all the way, but this was the worst. We finally reached the top of a mountain and settled down for the night. The next day we were hot and dry. My tongue was actually swollen. I'd seen that in the movies and read about it, but I guess I'd never been convinced such things happened. And my lips were cracked. I'd had that happen as a kid, so I wasn't surprised. I found that water, and orange juice, and ice-cold Coca-Cola were all I thought about for minutes on end.

One of the men came up to me. "Hey, chaplain, wasn't there a story in the Bible about a guy who hit a rock and water came out?"

"Yeah," I said, smiling as much as my cracked lips would allow. "Moses did that."

"Well, why don't you try it, chaplain?"

I don't remember saying anything. I just looked at him, and found the smile on my face getting wider, and then fading. As we moved out, I said, "Lord, help us." I didn't have faith enough for anything else.

It was no more than four minutes later when we filed into a clearing and there before us was a gigantic rock with a pool of sparkling water cut into the top. I turned to the man who had spoken to me. "There you are." I pointed with exaggeration, but with seriousness. The man's face was solemn for several seconds, and then a wide grin broke across it.

God's Spirit was moving in the Third Battalion. More and more men were coming to services and asking Jesus to come and live with them. A new briefing shack was built and the services in the rear were crammed full with officers and enlisted men. I was going hard, and many mornings I found my bones ached as I roused myself.

One morning I woke early and was asking the Lord to move even more sweepingly upon the men on the battlefield. "Father," I said, "I'm going to fast today, asking you to pour out your Spirit in even greater abundance across the whole battalion."

At midafternoon, I had a piercing headache. "I'm not very good at this fasting business," I said to myself, assuming I was suffering the effects of not eating. I pressed on. That night I woke in the middle of the night. My body was perspiring but I was ice cold; chills streaked across me. I finally dropped off to sleep again, and the next day I struggled up and prayed on.

It was Saturday, and because of a military operation scheduled for the next day, we held our worship service that night. As I preached, I felt as though I were in some kind of a trance. My mind was locked. The room began to spin and I feared I would collapse in front of everyone. Our doctor was there, and after the services I asked him to take a look at me. He checked me over, took a blood sample, and said very little except, "I'll let you know."

Later that night, he came to my tent. "Curry, you have vivax malaria."

"I can't have!" I almost shouted from my bunk. "I've never missed a pill. I just can't have it!"

"Well, friend, you have malaria. Period. You'll have to go to Nha Trang Hospital tomorrow afternoon." He spoke gently, aware of the pain I was in, mentally as well as physically. The word had gone out to commanders to cut down on malaria, or else. Our troops had been overwhelmingly plagued by it. It was stated further that if the men took the pills, they definitely would not get malaria. So anyone who fell ill with it was in trouble with his commander.

The next morning I told my boss and, as I feared, he exploded. "You've got what?" I was silent. His voice eased in a moment. "How could you have it?"

I could only shrug and shake my head. I felt I'd really let him down.

Later in the morning, I had a strong urge to go to the Vietnamese church at nearby Bao Loc. I'd met the pastor when I first arrived and had immediately liked him.

"Brother," I said with a weak smile, "do you believe in James 5:14?" He didn't speak English, but I opened his Vietnamese Bible and pointed to the verse. He nodded his head vigorously, his face aglow with a smile. I finally made him understand I was sick—really all he had to do was look at me and see that—and wanted him to pray for me. He nodded his head vigorously again.

At one point in his Sunday morning service, he motioned for me to come forward. I weakly obeyed, kneeling in front of the small, poor congregation. The pastor anointed my forehead with oil, and I was immediately surrounded by warmth. It entered me—I was positive of it—and passed through my body. I couldn't understand the words the pastor or the others were speaking, but I knew in my spirit what they were asking of the Lord. I began to thank Jesus and praise Him. I knew He had touched me, answering the prayers of these small, dark-skinned, humble people, thousands of miles from my homeland. I unashamedly let the tears roll down my face and onto the floor.

The rough, hot ride to Nha Trang aboard a C-123 was the worst I had taken. There I felt more like a POW than an officer in uniform as the doctors and orderlies shoved me from one place to another until I landed in a nice air-conditioned hospital ward and fell into the softness of a clean bed. Before long I looked like a heroin addict; needle holes covered my arms. The ward assistants, nurses, and doctors ran countless tests on me, and by the end of the fourth day they had found nothing. There was no trace of malaria, and I felt fine. I knew the Lord had healed me.

But the pill failures puzzled me as well as the doctors, and the search went on. At last they concluded that the little pills, with their hard outer shell, had been going through my body so rapidly that I was getting no protection. It was a fluke between me and the pills that was remedied after more testing by my breaking the pills and thus defeating the outer shell.

Despite my healing and the enjoyment of my rest, I was

moving quickly toward depression over my absence from my ministry. How could it continue with me so far away in the hospital? I feared all my hard work would go down the drain. Finally it occurred to me that I had forgotten my own words from Romans 8:28 to the men in the field: ". . . all things work together for good. . . ."

After the fifth day in the hospital—when I knew that the Lord had healed me, but the doctors didn't—I got up and went for a walk along the corridor. "Lord," I prayed semi-audibly, "you know how much I love you. Now I'm going to turn this whole ministry over to you. I've been acting as though it were my ministry. I will thank you if I have to spend the rest of my tour in this hospital."

Immediately, the discouragement lifted. The prayer had taken things from my hands and put them into the Lord's, where He could do something about them. Two days later, the doctors became convinced I was well and were satisfied with the broken-pill remedy.

I headed back to Bao Loc and the Lord's ministry.

6

SYMBOLS

"What's that you're doing?" asked Earl, a Southern Baptist missionary serving at nearby Dalat.

"I'm putting out flowers for our new chapel," I said.

"New chapel? What chapel?" He laughed.

"The one that's going right there." I pointed to the little plot of bare ground. "It'll have the front door right where the back of my tent is. I'm going to trust the Lord to give us a chapel, and these flowers are the symbol of my faith. See it?"

"I *see* it!" he exclaimed.

For several minutes in the blistering sun I told Earl my feelings about the need for a chapel and the recent progress, and the delays, in meeting that need.

Many men in the battalion had come to know Jesus and needed not only a place to worship, but also a symbol of their faith. Almost every day I spoke to someone, around the compound or out in the field, about the dream. Many were excited about it.

But lumber was a problem. It was almost impossible to get.

So, gradually learning my lessons, I committed the problem to the Lord and prayed and thanked Him daily about it. It wasn't long before the supply officer told me that, without question, the chapel was the next priority on his list. The battalion commander agreed.

The next day, as I sat in my tent, I heard people shouting. It took two or three seconds for me to pick up the words. "Fire! Fire!" I jumped up to look out, and saw bright flames leaping fifty feet into the air. There was more shouting. "It's the mess hall!" I ran to get a closer look. It was the mess hall all right. Ugly flames were shooting out from all sides.

After the blaze was put out, I silently thanked the Lord that no one had been hurt, but deep inside, I was disappointed, even a bit resentful. I knew what it meant: the lumber designated for the chapel would have to go for a new mess hall. It made sense, but I was still upset.

Once again, I managed to turn the disappointment over to the Lord before it got out of control. "I trust you, Lord," I whispered under my breath as I stared at the ruined hall.

Several days later, at the end of a two-day walk with my old friends in Charlie Company, First Sergeant Villagomez looked out over a stream and pointed to some Vietnamese lily bulbs. "Chaplain," he said, "do you want to get some flowers for the new chapel that's going to be built?" His faith was still obviously strong, lumber or not.

"Why, yes, I guess so, but how?"

The next thing I knew, he and some of the soldiers were digging up bulbs and loading them into empty sandbags. We carried them out to the landing zone where the helicopters were to pick us up for our return to Camp Rock.

The men dropped the bags off in front of my tent and it was then that Earl, whose car had broken down at Bao Loc, came upon me with shovel in hand. He understood the vision, and before long we were praising and thanking the Lord together for the new chapel that was to be flanked by lovely flowers.

I drew up plans for a chapel, with a library, living quarters, and an office in the rear. The next step was uncertain. But one day a group of engineers arrived to survey the area. Could it be we were on our way? They were able to complete only part of the job that day, and then a higher-priority job interfered.

I stood in front of the area two days later with my chin in my hand and pondered the problem. "I can do this sort of stuff," I mumbled aloud but to myself. Surely I had retained some of the knowledge pounded into me at West Point. So I borrowed one of the instruments used to line up mortars and artillery and set out to try to finish the surveying job. Hallelujah! It worked.

Then, another miracle. Enough lumber was left over from the mess hall for us to begin. It arrived unexpectedly one morning, and down went the timbers for the foundation. My plans worked! Then up went the walls. It was happening! "The Lord is building himself a temple of worship," I said as I watched.

The camp was buzzing with excitement. There would soon be a chapel! When I went to the field, the men soaked up details of progress. One payday, a commander in the field, a young blond lieutenant, came up to me, thrust out his fist, and crammed a wad of bills into my hand. I could hardly hold it with both hands.

"What's this?" I asked.

"That's to buy some pews with, chaplain," he said, serious-faced but obviously happy. "Some of the men out here want to help with the building of the chapel."

Tears filled my eyes. The young lieutenant understood and walked away as I stood speechless. God was very present on that battlefield.

The sisters of the Sao Mai Roman Catholic orphanage nearby came to tell me they wanted to pay for our altar and pulpit, and directed me to a wood craftsman in town who could build it. I had just about enough money to have the project finished, pews and all, so I set a target date of Pentecost Sunday, just two weeks away, for our first service in the new chapel.

Bill, my assistant, and others picked up hammers whenever they could and pounded nails just about daily. Meanwhile, I continued to go to and from the field for daily services. As much as I wanted to see the chapel completed, I knew my primary job was to minister in the field, telling men about Jesus and leading them to Him.

Just as the roof of the chapel building was completed, the monsoon season began. Water streamed constantly into our leaky tent. So as soon as possible, Bill and I moved into our new quarters at the rear of the nearly completed building. It wasn't the Waldorf, but we saw it as a king's palace. That very first night, a torrent came down. I snuggled up in my bedroll and listened. It was beautiful. The tin roof and wooden walls, and that luxurious wooden floor, were far better than a canvas tent and dirt floors.

Our Vietnamese craftsman wasn't the speediest in the world, and on the night before our grand opening, when we went for the furniture, a number of finishing touches were still needed. We huddled, and decided to take it as it was. The finishing touches could be added after installation.

The furniture was in place, and everything was beautiful, right down to the little brass bell from the Sao Mai sisters that would summon the men to worship. And we even had a small organ that had been brought in from Cam Rahn Bay. Our organist wasn't skilled enough to master the keys for that first service, but he could keep us in time with the bass foot pedal.

From the rising of the morning sun to the last flickering light of day, God gave us beautiful weather on Pentecost Sunday. The brightly painted sign out front welcomed men from all over the camp to the "Rock Memorial Chapel." And it was filled—double our normal attendance. Our little building, built in war-torn desolation, was bursting at the seams with just what it was designed for—worship.

And that's the way it went week after week. Men came from all over to worship God in that small, simple setting. And as the days moved on, it took on a more polished look. It was painted white, and one man built a little white picket fence for the front. Others laid a gravel sidewalk and planted grass and more flowers. The Vietnamese lilies flourished.

Sadness mingled with our optimism the last Sunday in August. It was our final service in Rock Memorial Chapel. Word had come down from headquarters that the compound was being dismantled and the battalion moved to Landing Zone Uplift, nearly three hundred miles north. We had no options. We were moving, and I was convinced God would not let those Camp Rock miracles go to waste. He would take care of us.

But it was unnerving that last Sunday morning. The engineers had come to the service with their wrecking tools in hand. At the final "amen," they began knocking the walls down. In no more than an hour, our lovely house of worship was a pile of wood.

We loaded the pews, altar, and pulpit on two platforms so they could be taken north. I had been told all of it would go by land to Cam Rahn Bay, be loaded onto the ship for Qui Nhon, and then carried by truck to Landing Zone Uplift. At the last minute, I was given word that some space was available on one of the cargo planes, and I was able to send one of the platforms on ahead.

Two weeks earlier, I had been given a new assistant—Ken—as Bill was reassigned, and together we fasted and prayed in preparation for the move. We didn't eat or drink for three days. "Lord God," we cried in numerous variations, "we call upon you to meet every need of your people and to expand this ministry at the new camp."

Our move went smoothly. One of the first things I was told when I arrived was that a platform loaded with some of our pews was off in one corner of the compound. Rejoicing, I rushed over and found them to be in excellent condition. The altar and pulpit had also fared well.

The process of moving into a new area for our base camp was difficult. Telephones, electrical wiring, latrines, a mess hall, and living quarters had to be set up. At the same time, the combat troops were moving into their new area of operations. And, from my standpoint, I had not only to establish a place to live, but also to carry on with the ministry, especially in the field.

For the first time during my Vietnam tour, I had the opportunity to work closely with a Roman Catholic chaplain. The priests had been in short supply and had only visited camp periodically. But now, Father Halleran and I were responsible for the men of two battalions, the First and the Third. And while we were together, the role of combat troops went from the "search and destroy" missions to "pacification." This meant our troops were living in and around villages to keep the enemy out and to help the people build up their own defenses and communities. Some locations had only squad-sized units (eleven men) stationed in them.

In all, we had thirty-eight sites in the two battalions. On a good day, we could cover four and five units, and would each average fifteen to twenty services a week, conducting them simultaneously. It was a good learning experience for both of us, proving to me that Catholics and Protestants could and should work together, as was being learned in civilian life in the United States, particularly in several ecumenical Christian communities.

I found myself falling in and out of helicopters, moving in on days when the units received fresh rations, and fatigue sank deeper and deeper into my body. But the Lord never failed to give me the strength to get to the field. He knew the importance of those moments to the men.

In the midst of setting up a new place to live in and a new area of ministry, I was often asked about the prospects for a new chapel—a new symbol. There was a tiny chapel at Uplift, but it was far too small to accommodate all those who wanted to attend. My first thought was to take the used materials and reconstruct the Rock Memorial Chapel. That, I soon found out, was impossible. First, I was told that our lumber was needed for new barracks. But then, I learned that our other platform load of pews had come in. They were nothing but kindling. We had only a pile of broken wood. Nothing was worth salvaging.

However, the Lord undertook again, with holy imagination.

A close examination of the little chapel at Uplift showed it had a plywood floor. And it was made of 1-by-6-inch lumber on the outside, and had 2-by-8 beams of 16-foot length overhead and 1-by-6 boards to add a decorative effect. I went down to the lumberyard one day and found seventy-five new 2-by-8, 16-foot beams along with several huge stacks of 1-by-8 lumber. By replacing the 1-by-6 beams on the outside of the chapel with 1-by-8, we had enough 1-by-6 beams for the inside. We were then given enough lightweight plywood to panel the inside and cover the floor.

With that, my faithful assistant, Ken, went to work. We added an extension to the old chapel that would double our seating capacity. The lumber matched perfectly. The inside and outside were painted white, and fluorescent lights were added.

For the front door, we were getting ready to use two regular doors side by side, one opening in, the other out. But at the last minute, the engineer sergeant said he had a regular theater-style double door that would be perfect. He was right. It put the final touch on the building.

The little brass bell from Bao Loc went into the bell tower, the still-new altar and pulpit were installed in front, newly constructed pews were alternated with the old ones, and we were in business again. A Korean tailor shop even provided us with a maroon curtain for the rear.

Ken and I stood back and looked at everything. "Lord," I said aloud, "I've never seen a prettier chapel anywhere. You've put everything into place perfectly. And we want to thank you."

We had had a need at Camp Rock. The Lord had provided. We had developed a new need at Landing Zone Uplift. The Lord had provided.

As before, the men responded immediately. Hundreds from the field came in to share in our services when they were brought to the base camp for periodic short stays. The symbol of faith was once more visible.

Several of the men confronted me one morning shortly after the completion of the chapel.

"Chaplain," one said, "several of us have mentioned to you our need for Bible study, and we'd like to state that need again and ask you to help us. Some of us have gotten very close to the Lord in recent weeks, and we feel a need to get deeper into His Word. Most of us have no background in that sort of thing, and we want to do something about it."

Determination was visible in their faces. I was a little embarrassed that they had had to initiate such an effort. It usually worked the other way around.

We immediately began meeting every evening that I was in the camp area, usually in the chapel, sometimes in my tent.

Most of the time there were only four or five of us, but we were earnest, meeting often past midnight, poring over one book of Scripture after another.

One of the men who attended regularly was named George. He had drifted away from the Lord, but had recently rededicated his life. He read the Bible day and night and sought with all his might to grow in his faith. He was an MP, and I'd often see him at his gatepost reading his Bible. I had never encountered anyone more ardent. In a short time, he, along with all the others in that little group, received the baptism with the Holy Spirit.

George became a very powerful man in the Scriptures before long. He was an invaluable friend and ally. One night early in the Bible studies, I noticed he was jotting something down on a notepad. He continued night after night. Finally, I asked him, "George, what's that you're writing down?"

"All the Scripture references you quote," he said.

"Why?"

"Because I wanted to check you out and see if you were giving us the straight stuff." He smiled broadly. "You were."

"Oh." It had never occurred to me that anyone would be checking up on me; it was a relief to know I hadn't messed up. I was grateful to the Holy Spirit for keeping me straight in the midst of all our frenzy. I was grateful, too, to have a colleague who was growing so strong in the Bible.

That same night, George told us he was witnessing to the Vietnamese interpreter who worked with our MPs. We immediately began to pray for the man, and before long George rushed in a minute or two late one night. He was breathless, and beaming. "He did it!"

"Did what?" we chorused.

"He asked Jesus into his life!"

I'd never seen George happier. He described every detail to us. "I told him about Jesus and finally I asked him if he wanted

Jesus to come into his life. He told me he did, so I told him to get down on his knees, raise his hands into the air, and shout at the top of his voice, 'Jesus, come into my life!' "

I winced. "Was it necessary to have him shout?" I asked.

"Don't knock it, chaplain." He laughed. "I was ashamed of Jesus for the first few years after I had asked Him into my life, and I wanted my friend to get off on the right foot."

As I ministered day after day in the field, I recognized more and more of the men from the individual units, and in some cases I remembered their names. And then, from time to time, a familiar face would be missing. Invariably it meant that the man had been killed or wounded since my last visit—something I never got used to.

Each time this happened—and it started to happen more and more often—it drove me deeper into the conviction that I had to present Christ more aggressively than ever before. I resolved to give an invitation to receive the Lord Jesus at the end of every sermon I preached and to do everything else I could to lead those men to a simple prayer of faith and acceptance of Jesus into their lives. I realized more than ever the seriousness of the situation I was in. I had been well trained for leadership of combat forces against the Communist aggressors of the earth, but I had been woefully untrained for the greater struggle against "principalities, against powers, against the rulers of the darkness of this world, against spiritual wickedness in high places" (Eph. 6:12). That was warfare of the highest order, fought on a battleground with an added dimension.

But I was learning. I was seeing that the enemy was the devil himself—that the horrors of famine, pollution, human greed and cruelty, gross perversions of every sort, and the cold death of much organized religion were his handiwork.

At the same time, I was seeing that as strong as that enemy

was, as horrible as his powers were, he was utterly defenseless in the face of God's power. Jesus was supreme. And the people must be told that—civilians and soldiers alike. I was learning.

One Sunday night at an evening service in the camp, I gave my regular invitation, and a man named Gordan responded. After he had prayed and accepted Christ to become part of his life, he said, "Chaplain, I was a philosophy major in college. I thought I had the whole business of life and death all figured out. Then I began to read the Bible, and my logic didn't fit in with what I read. But I just couldn't refute what I read. It was there before me, and all I could do was accept it."

Gordan became a regular member of our fellowship. He was in the reconnaissance platoon and often had to go out on very dangerous missions. He was scared, but we prayed frequently about it, and he grew steadily in his faith. I really loved him—he was so honest—and I knew God loved him even more than I did.

One day a few weeks after Gordan had begun his walk in faith, I was told that a medivac helicopter was coming in. I headed toward the aid station, not knowing what was ahead of me. I always found this part of my ministry the most difficult. Our men were constantly running into booby traps, and the results were devastating. I was torn deep inside as I ministered to those young men screaming in agony over the loss of a leg or an arm. I never handled it well.

"One man is dead and three wounded, chaplain," one of the medics said as he walked into the station. "The bird is inbound; be here in about zero three."

In just a few moments I heard the "whup whup" of the helicopter in the distance. Every second was tense. The doctors and medics were waiting with everything in the way of life-saving devices. I paced.

Abruptly the helicopter landed. The medics rushed out and carried stretchers with the wounded into the station. Then I saw them unload the brown body bag. It had become an all-too-familiar sight.

"Who is it?" I asked.

"A man by the name of Logan," the medic said. "Know him, chaplain?"

The words roared in my mind, but I was silent. "Know him? Know him? I loved him! He was my brother!" Then I spoke aloud, "Gordan Logan from recon?"

"Yes, chaplain, that's him."

I watched as they took him to a far, dark corner of the aid station and laid his body on the cold floor. Everyone was concerned, as they should have been, with the wounded men on the tables. The doctors worked expertly, quietly. I spoke a few words with the pain-wracked men, trying as hard as I could to console them, but truthfully my heart was with Gordan at that moment.

Finally, I walked over and looked down. They had opened the bag and there he lay—still, without life. One small particle of metal from a hand grenade booby trap had gone directly into his heart. "It was all over very quickly, chaplain," a doctor told me.

I looked down at my friend. "Well, Gordan, I'm going to miss you. But I know you're with the King now. You're in good hands. I'll see you again one day."

In the dark corner, I wept in sorrow for the loss of such a friend, a brother, in such a pointless way, but still, I rejoiced. He had conquered death through Christ.

Sometimes the building of those chapels seemed futile and difficult—maybe even silly. But then I remembered George, and Gordan, and so many others like them, and I remembered that those simple little structures were symbols of their faith, symbols of who they really were.

And that's the way it went.

Cadet Vaughan

Curry and Nancy Vaughan, just after their wedding 5 June 1963.

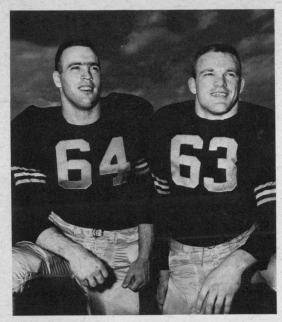

Curry and his brother Gwynn. Both were varsity football players at West Point. Gwynn was a year behind Curry.

Curry and Nancy Vaughan.

Some of the boys in Alpha. Bucky is in middle front.

Rock Memorial Chapel.

Rapping in Vietnam.

Service in the field.

7

FAITH

Easter and the Bravo Lima tragedy were behind us when the commander of Alpha Company asked if I'd like to go out on a night patrol. Many of the officers were pleased when I accompanied the men in the field. Some believed in what I was preaching; others saw me as an insurance policy; some a good luck charm. I was quite sure this commander, Captain Wass de Czega, had the Lord in mind.

It was described as a dangerous mission, right into the midst of the Viet Cong. I was not as brave as I sounded when I quickly responded to his invitation. "Sure. I'd like it."

A hundred of us set out from trucks right after dark. We were to circle and come in from the other side onto an old tea plantation once owned by the French. A force of VC were believed to be holed up there.

We climbed quietly down from the trucks that had carried us to our starting point and moved out. "Hey, this is nice," I thought. The ground was level and firm. As I walked along, my mind toyed with the Scripture that said we Christians should "pray without ceasing" (1 Thess. 5:17). "That's a tough one," I thought, "but it sure ought to apply here." The Bravo Lima tragedy was fresh in my mind, and the cleverness of the enemy in the jungle could never be forgotten.

I shuffled along in the line of one hundred men with my air mattress, my rucksack, and my little chaplain's kit. I carried no weapon. The night was growing very dark. "Lord, I think I'd like to try 'walking in the Spirit' throughout this whole mission." I was moving my lips as I talked, but no one could hear me. "I'd like to stay in communion with you the whole time."

Quite easily and simply I began to pray, mostly in tongues, to myself. I was going to pray that way the whole night, the Lord willing.

All of a sudden, we hit the swamps. We had no lights and we just plowed in. I continued to pray in tongues, but other thoughts raced through my mind. "Wow! This is work." I was immediately up to my neck in water and goo. And I knew the leeches were latching onto my legs and body. I reached up and there was one on my neck. Ugh! It was black and gooey, big and sucking. It clung and pulled at my skin as I tore it off. Without interruption, I praised the Lord in tongues. I worshiped Him and thanked Him, even while I was reacting in disgust to the swamp and the leeches.

Just like all the other men, I pushed on, stepping carefully to avoid holes and a plunge over my head, ever mindful of the hundreds of snakes all around us. I shifted into English for a moment. "Lord, I ask you to bless these men. Direct their steps. Take care of them." And back into tongues.

I had no idea how many hours passed, but it was a long time. Then, we were out of the swamp and onto dry ground. Making as little noise as possible, we stopped long enough to get the ugly leeches off. They were literally all over us. Then we pushed on with our big circle—over the hills and then the fields and finally without incident right into our destination.

The VC had gone! We had secured the place without a battle. "Thank you, Lord." I continued praying.

The commander was there, having come in from the other side. He looked curiously at me as we approached. The men were filthy and dragging after fourteen hours of hard work and strain.

"Chaplain," Wass de Czega said, still looking at me rather strangely, "you look great after that hike. You look really fresh. How come you're not all worn out like the others?"

"It was the Lord," I said smiling. Little did he know!

"How did you like it?" he asked, letting my remark pass.

"It was fine—tough, but fine." I continued to smile.

I joined the other men to wait for the helicopters to take us back to the base. Sitting on the ground, I poked little holes into the dirt with my forefinger. "The Scripture really works, doesn't it, Lord?" I shook my head and was aware that I was grinning from ear to ear.

It was night, and the monsoon season was approaching, but the air was cool and quite comfortable. Much of the time the weather was like that of a tropical island, steaming hot in the daytime but cool and breezy in the evenings. That's the way it was that night in the fall of 1969.

I had flown in by helicopter to the tiny village in the north to spend the night with the nine men stationed there to protect it during the Vietnamization process. It was a small compound, sandbagged all around. It was a very sandy place, right alongside a big lake. As I swept my eyes across the open area, I was aware only of rice paddies everywhere and little Vietnamese huts breaking the skyline behind us.

It was getting dark fast. We had finished eating, and I moved from man to man, talking to them about anything they wanted to talk about. Most of them eventually raised the subject of

God, and I encouraged and reassured them at every opportunity. I climbed up on top of a big sand dune and sat down beside a young, dark-haired fellow. I never did know his name.

"Hello," I spoke softly in the darkness. "I'm Chaplain Vaughan. How are things going?"

He was shy, but friendly. We talked about how dull things had been even though they knew the enemy was out there, a constant threat. And we talked about his home, somewhere in the middle of the United States.

"Do you think about God?" I asked.

"Yes, sir," he said. "I think about Him a lot, particularly at night." He paused. "I've attended some of your services out here."

"Have you ever accepted Christ as your Lord and Savior?" It was easy in those Vietnam settings to drive right to the point.

"No, sir." He was quiet. "But I've heard you talk about that."

"Well listen, friend, you know God is here with you, right in this messed-up situation. He's here, and you can know Him, and be His, and live with Him. He not only will live with you right here, but He'll give you eternal life, so that you will live with Him forever, no matter what happens."

The night was very quiet. I was conscious only of cricket sounds in the distance. In the darkness I couldn't make out the expression on his face, but I knew he was serious. It was a critical moment.

"Would you like that?" I asked after ten seconds. "Would you like to ask Jesus Christ to come into your life, literally into your heart, to forgive you your sins and to live in you, and to bring you into communion with Him and the Father?" I waited five more seconds. "Would you like to become a follower of Christ?"

I knew he was wrestling. And I was glad. I didn't want to push too far. I had to let him make the decision.

"Yes, chaplain, I'd like that. It's been in my mind for two or three weeks. I want to know God. I want to belong to Christ."

"Thank you, Lord." I spoke to myself. Then I placed my hand on the boy's shoulder and spoke aloud. "Okay, brother, it can be done right here, right now. Why don't you and I pray together?"

"Okay."

I led him in a prayer of confession and acceptance of Jesus into his life. It was simple and quiet. I'm sure no one in the little compound knew exactly what was happening.

Without warning, machine gun fire split the night. Bullets whizzed over our heads, seemingly inches away. The boy and I rolled off the dune down into the compound, lying flat. The frightening, staccato sounds turned the moment into chaos.

Suddenly, it was over. And everything was silent once again. The silence seemed deeper. "Praise you, Jesus." I spoke the words aloud and turned to the boy. We pushed ourselves up from the ground.

"You know, if one of those rounds had caught you, you'd be in heaven now."

He turned to look directly at me. "Yes, sir, I know. I thought about that."

I was close enough to see him smiling in the darkness.

Manuel was a good-looking young Spanish guy, very kind and tender-hearted, but a courageous soldier. Everyone in the unit liked him, and showed it. He was due to become an American citizen soon, and he was extraordinarily proud of that. He talked of almost nothing else.

One day he was brought into the aid station. Both of his legs had been blown off above the knee by a booby trap. I saw him briefly, but he was in no condition to talk. After initial treatment he was sent immediately to the evacuation hospital thirty minutes away by helicopter.

I was able a few days later to fly down to the hospital. I talked to Manuel. He was so typical of many of our guys—proud to be serving his country, even in an unpopular war. We talked about his impending citizenship, and tears came into his eyes, even though he continued to smile. And we talked about his imminent return to the States, and about things back at the unit. We talked about the Lord, and prayed.

Six weeks later, we received a newspaper clipping from Manuel. It was an article about his swearing-in, and a picture showed him standing. The article said the judge had suggested he sit down because of the obvious pain he was suffering on his new artificial legs. He had just been fitted, and the pain was excruciating.

"No, sir, I'll stand," Manuel replied firmly, a smile creasing his handsome face.

I knew this was a difficult time for Nancy, but in many ways it was extremely important for both of us. It constantly forced us to examine ourselves in relation to one another, in relation to the Lord and to what He was doing. For the most part we communicated by tape recording, using little reels about the size of cassettes that held thirty minutes of talk. This proved to be far more profound than letter writing. We could hear one another—the inflections, the loneliness, the anger, the laughter, the crying. We talked to each other as we never had before. There was no time for frills, no time to waste on nonessentials. We spoke of love and relationship at every level. We spoke of marriage and children, of living and dying. I poured my heart into the tapes about the need to present Christ to every person, the need to show the way to salvation and eternal life.

I was keenly aware that Nancy was often confused about my

Holy Spirit experience. She had not entered into the ministry with the miraculous gifts of the Spirit. She had not spoken in tongues. And I knew she was still troubled with memories of my antics right after receiving the baptism with the Holy Spirit.

One day I received a tape in which she sobbed about her fears for our future life and ministry. She had a mental picture of me with my sleeves rolled up, a wild look in my eye, sweat pouring from my forehead, with my hands laid on some crippled person, screaming out for Jesus to heal him. On the tape I sent to her that day—we sent them daily—I prayed for God to show her that I was the same person she had loved and married seven years before. I asked the Lord to overcome the problem of our separation, the heavy load she was carrying with our two little children, the difficulties of living with her father.

Before long, I was able to follow that tape with a trip to Hawaii for five days of rest and recreation, joined by Nancy. We met at the R and R Center in Honolulu and embraced. We were like newlyweds, skipping from the exotic eating places to the beautiful beaches and surf. We soon realized how deep our lives had grown together, even during our separation. We knew we were in the hands of God and He would preserve us. I knew Nancy was no longer afraid.

Not long after I was baptized with the Holy Spirit, Bob Crick had told me I faced a choice. I could either continue to run in shallow water or step out in faith into the deeper water. "If you choose the latter," he had said, "after you've stepped out and you're over your head, go on out where it's really deep, because you can drown as easily in ten feet of water as you can in a thousand."

The further I moved into deep water, the more aware of the

spiritual world I became. Things I had before passed off as "circumstances" or "luck" became obviously related to "powers" and "principalities." The irritable boss or friend was not the problem. The problem was on the spiritual plane. Virtually all of life had some spiritual underpinning, as I had begun to see earlier, and it was still very difficult to make the transition from seeing things only on the flesh-and-blood level to recognizing the spiritual level.

As I wrestled with this and its application to my life in Vietnam, the simplest illustration I came up with was the time Peter walked on water (Matt. 14:28ff). There he got out of the boat, *believing Jesus had called him*, and he walked by faith. As long as he believed, and as long as he concentrated on Jesus, he was able to defy the natural laws of the world, which said his body would sink into the water. He was able to do something supernatural because he believed. Every step he took was a step of faith.

It was then I saw that, by faith, God's people could—when God called—overcome the natural, the flesh-and-blood obstacles of the world, which seemed to dictate our every move. When Peter began to look at the natural things—the harsh wind, the wild waves, and the flimsy, man-made boat—he lost faith, and fear struck his heart. The natural, earthly order and laws took over. Peter sank. Jesus rebuked him for his lack of faith and his doubt.

Faith conquers and assures us of real victory that could not otherwise be possible. Without faith, in fact, it is not possible to please God (Heb. 11:6).

And that's what God wanted to teach me in Vietnam. He wanted to begin to teach me to walk by faith in dealing with both the natural and the supernatural worlds—and He chose the fields of combat on which to do it.

It was during those days on that special battleground that I really had to come to grips with God on the fine details. Did I believe Him, or did I not? Did I believe—actually know—that He *was* with me? Could I *experience* that He was truly in charge of my life? Could I trust Him for even the little things?

In my case, the little things seemed often to center on transportation—getting around. I soon began to perceive that He was providing me with transportation to and from the places He wanted me, even when there was not supposed to be any transportation. One day near the end of my tour I calculated that there had been only one time when I was caught out in the field when I hadn't planned to stay out. That was in the middle of the monsoons, and I spent three extra days with Bravo Company on an unscheduled walk. Of course, that allowed me to minister to men I would not otherwise have been able to be with.

I was in Phan Thiet on the coast one day when I received word from my unit that my assistant, Ken, was scheduled to undergo surgery the next day at the hospital in Cam Rahn Bay. A tumor had been found in his chest. I felt I should go to see him, but it was five P.M. Officials told me there would be no more aircraft flying that night; I night possibly get out the next day. That would be too late. I whispered a prayer, thanking Jesus for the fact that He would provide a way.

I walked over to the chapel at the base and put a call through to Nancy on the Military Affiliate Radio Station, known as MARS. Just as I was finishing the call, I looked out the door and saw a giant C-130 coming down the runway. I ran as fast as I could as it got to the end of the airstrip. The rear door dropped and the loadmaster came out.

"Where are you going?" I yelled over the roar of the engines.

"Cam Rahn Bay!" came the shout.

"Praise the Lord! Can I go with you?"

"Yes!"

I got on board and the door shut behind me. In a moment, we were rolling down the runway and were airborne. I sat down in the cargo area, which held a length of huge drainage pipe. The loadmaster soon came by and asked if I'd like to move up front with the pilots. I gladly moved out of the rear area, with its hot, humid air and foul odors. Up front, I was served a cold Coke in air-conditioned comfort.

As the airplane leveled off and we headed north, I watched the sunset streaking the sky off on the horizon. "Why did you come by here?" I asked.

The pilot chuckled. "We tried to tell control headquarters that the Phan Thiet airstrip would be closed, but they insisted that we come on down anyway. We had to go ahead and land. We were supposed to unload this pipe."

I merely nodded. There had been no plane scheduled for that evening, but God knew I needed to be in Cam Rahn Bay, and He knew I had faith to believe Him for it. So He sent a four-engine C-130 to pick me up.

At Cam Rahn Bay, I didn't know how to find Ken and the hospital. It was a much bigger place than I'd expected. Just outside the aircraft, I stopped and looked around. "Lord, you provided me a way here, and I know you'll provide me a way to where I'm going and a place to spend the night."

I left the C-130 and walked through the big, busy air terminal filled with tired-looking soldiers going to and coming from the battlefields. I asked a sergeant how I might get to the hospital and was told a regular bus went by the front of the terminal. I went out, found a bus waiting, and got on. Without planning it, I sat next to an air force chaplain. He had watched me getting on the bus.

"Where are you heading?" he asked immediately.

"I'm going to the hospital to see my assistant. He's supposed to have surgery tomorrow." I wanted in the worst way to ask about a place to stay, but instead I silently told the Lord I was trusting Him to lead me to the perfect place.

As that little prayer went up, the chaplain asked, "Where are you staying tonight?"

"I don't have a place," I responded.

"I'll tell you what, I'll take you to the BOQ [bachelor officers' quarters], get you a room, and then take you to the hospital."

I'm sure a smile was spread clear across my face. "That's very kind of you. I'd appreciate it." I spoke silently to Jesus, "Thank you, Lord."

I was soon with Ken, and we prayed fervently about the tumor in his chest. I found myself thanking God that he was going to take care of it. (The tumor was removed the following day, and it was benign.)

Meanwhile, I learned that to catch a helicopter back to my base, I had to get to an airport an hour from the BOQ. I'd have to get up at three-thirty A.M. and find a ride at that crazy hour. I had no alarm clock. As I fell into my bed, exhausted, I prayed, "Lord Jesus, you know I'm dead on my feet. If you want me back tomorrow, you'll not only have to wake me up, but also give me strength to get out of bed."

I woke in absolute darkness and looked at my watch's luminous dial. Three-forty-five. My whole body screamed as I commanded it to get up. I barely made it, but I *did* make it, and with fifteen minutes' more sleep than I'd expected.

I went out into the cool, predawn air and walked a block or so to the main road. There wasn't a sound. "How will I ever get to the airport?" I said into the silence. "Oh, well. Lord, I just thank you. You woke me up, and I know you'll get me there on time."

Just then, I heard a motor. It was a jeep. I recognized it as part of the base's security patrol. I waved, and it stopped. "I need a ride to the helicopter port," I said. "Can you help me?"

"Sure," the driver said, "we'll get you halfway there anyhow."

The jeep was the only vehicle in sight at that hour.

One ride later, in the back of a two-and-a-half-ton truck, I was in the pilots' mess hall eating a fine breakfast. We took off right on time in a big Chinook helicopter, and in an hour I was back home.

"This is amazing, Lord," I said, shaking my head. In less than twelve hours, during the time when no flights were scheduled, I had made my three-hundred-mile trip and done the things I believed God had called me to do. All that had been required of me was to believe that He would do what He said He would. He had given me a glimpse of what it could be like. But I needed to learn to see better, so He could take care of the big things and the little ones, too.

One afternoon, I began reading a book by Don Basham, *Face Up With a Miracle*. As I read, the Lord seemed to be trying to break through to me, to tell me something. The more I read, the more I felt the Spirit speaking to me. I sensed a deep love and felt the strength of God all through my body. But I didn't know what He was saying to me.

I put the book down and went next door to the chapel. Maybe prayer would open up the matter. Twenty minutes later, as I sat back down on my bed to continue reading, I sensed a struggle within me. I still didn't know what it was, so I started to read.

The first words I read were those describing the first time Basham publicly gave his testimony about his experiences with the Holy Spirit. I looked up from the book and spoke aloud. "Lord, is this what you want?"

A voice spoke within me. "Yes."

I immediately knew God wanted me to share with my denomination what had happened to me. The coldness of fear touched my arms and legs, and my scalp tingled. At that time, the Presbyterian, U.S. Church had little in its theology to deal with such experiences. I would be putting everything on the line if I spoke up. But I knew this was God's plan. It had to be done.

In the next twenty-four hours, in addition to my other duties, I wrote out a twenty-two-page paper. I was as honest and specific as I knew how. With real fear and actual trembling, I sent it to Nancy for typing and asked her to send it to my endorsing agent, a Presbyterian clergyman, and to my presbytery. I could well be a layman shortly.

In sending the paper, I was fulfilling my vows to the church. At ordination, I had promised that I would report any changes in my theology. But, with that paper, I was also reviving the burden Nancy had carried about our future. I knew the experience would be traumatic for her.

I personally felt a tremendous relief, and knew I had been obedient in taking the step. (I heard nothing for six months, not until I had returned to the United States, and then came a reply from the presbytery. A statement of reactions and recommendations concluded that the officials "saw no problem as long as I labored outside the bounds of presbytery." Well, at least I was still a chaplain! Not long after I had received the letter, the General Assembly of the church adopted a position, which it now holds, stating that "while this is not the 'normal' experience, it did happen." I disagreed with the position, but nonetheless shouted aloud to Nancy: "Praise the Lord! I've gone from being a heretic to being abnormal.")

My emotions were deeply mixed the day in 1970 that I left Vietnam. I felt sadness and melancholy at leaving so many fine young Americans trapped in that cruel war. It was far from over. But I felt a certain satisfaction and was very thankful for what I had seen in that one short year.

I sat in the Cam Rahn Bay airport awaiting my flight and stared at the little notebook I had kept since my arrival. It showed that I had seen more than four hundred soldiers bow their heads and ask Jesus into their lives. Some had acted in response to invitations, some through personal contact. They had been hungry to hear the gospel, as people always were in times of stress and heartache. War was no different. It pushed men to an awareness of their lostness.

I looked out the window at the countryside. Some of those men were in heaven right then because they had heard and accepted the Lord Jesus into their lives and then subsequently died on the battlefield. They lived on.

I remembered the conversation I had had several months earlier with a battle-scarred sergeant. "Chaplain." He had looked me square in the face. "Why do you stay in this business? You don't see any long-lasting results."

I had remained silent for several seconds. "No, sarge, you're wrong. There are good results."

I spoke on to myself as he moved on to another subject. "He just doesn't know. . . . The blind see. . . . The lame walk. . . . The evil one is cast out. . . . I don't always see the long-term results, but . . . ."

And I remembered the time the young lieutenant had asked me if I ever got mad at God over the war.

"No, Tom," I had replied. "I have never gotten mad. God isn't the one creating this pain and hurt and death and all these things. There's an enemy, and he's in charge of that department. God is not to blame for these things."

As the big jet rose from the runway and I saw the green and brown countryside, with the beautiful hills in the background, I remembered one by one the hundreds of ten-minute sermons I had delivered there—simple, little, straightforward talks. There had been no time for anything learned or sophisticated. The questions were too basic for that: "How can I come to know God?" "If I'm possibly going to get killed, how can I make sure I go to heaven?"

God had moved on the battleground. What was next?

8

TRUST

I was ready to leave kindergarten. Trust had been my major subject in Vietnam, and I had taken some significant steps. But they were, oh, so tiny in God's overall plan. Chapters three and four of the letter to the Hebrews spoke of where God was taking me if I was willing—and obedient. He was taking me into His "rest." But, first, I had to wrestle more with "trust."

After Vietnam, the Lord provided us with a three-bedroom home at Fort Bragg, near Fayetteville, North Carolina. That was a small miracle in itself. No housing had been available; then, when we arrived, there was one vacancy. And it was given to us. Nancy and I had merely joined hands and prayed, "Lord Jesus, you know every need we have, and you know the kind of house we need. We trust you to find us this house. Somewhere, there is a place just waiting for us, and we thank you for it."

As we were moving in, something happened to my back. At first, I took it to be fatigue, so I went into our bedroom to take a short nap. When I got up and walked, pain shot through my lower back like a flaming arrow. I fell to my knees, then staggered back to my feet, writhing in pain. Whether I was up or down, the pain was terrible.

I went to the dispensary. The doctor gave me some pills and said, "Drive on." By the time I got home I was almost paralyzed and had to crawl across the floor to get to the bed.

As cold sweat stood out on my forehead, I remembered the name of a surgeon at Fort Bragg who had been described as Spirit-filled. It was Gary Bluemink. I got to the telephone and called. It took two to three minutes for me to tell him who I was and to make plain I was a Jesus follower. He suddenly broke into my explanation. "Praise the Lord! Am I glad you're here!" I knew immediately that Gary loved Jesus, and we were one in the Spirit.

I told him of my predicament and he advised me to come to the hospital immediately. I wasn't sure I could, but I staggered out to the car, fell in, and Nancy drove me to the emergency room. I tried in vain to get out of the car. My body wouldn't respond. Two medics saw my problem and came running with a wheelchair. I was helpless.

Gary walked into the room, lean and smiling. But he wasted no time on introductions and small talk. He took me directly to a back specialist, who immediately admitted me to the hospital. I was in so much pain that I couldn't undress myself. Some soldier! I could only pray. "Praise you, Jesus. Thank you, Jesus."

After I was in bed, Gary came to my room, and then we talked. We definitely were one in the Spirit. And soon we prayed together, asking God directly for my healing. In an explosion of faith, I jumped out of bed and was able to stand for several seconds. It hurt. But from that point on, I believed—and voiced it—that I had been healed, and I thanked the Father for it.

Two days later, the pain was gone. My affliction had been diagnosed as severe sacroiliac strain, and I was given physical therapy, which undoubtedly helped. But I knew the author of my recovery. One of His names was the Great Physician.

In two more days I was out of the hospital. And a week later, I made my first parachute jump in seven years. The Lord had called me to minister to the First Brigade of the 82nd Airborne Division. It was airborne, and I had to be, too. So He made the way, and healed me.

All I had to do was trust.

My ministry to the troops and their families moved forward steadily, although much too slowly, but an old stumbling block in my personal life kept reappearing. It was my bad temper. The incidents at West Point with the wrestling coach and others had been meaningful. I had grown. But those, plus a certain amount of maturity, had only helped me to *control* my anger so I didn't act it out physically; the anger was still there. I was able to suppress it and internalize it to a great degree. And when I received the power of the Holy Spirit into my life things were better than ever, but in my deepest being—which I was starting to understand better—I still had a problem with my attitude. I had reached the point where I desperately wanted to change. But I could only pray.

Just before I left Vietnam, I had prayed about another problem. I had had fever blisters on my lips at least once a month for a long time. One night, in a surge of faith, I had said, "Lord, I thank you for all you've done in my life. Tonight, I'm going to claim in the name of Jesus that I will never again have a fever blister."

That was my last one for a year and a half. I was really rejoicing. Then one day, at Fort Bragg, I developed a large sore in my mouth. I rebuked it, and prayed against it, but there it was. I continued to praise the Lord for taking care of me, but I wondered why the problem had returned.

On Palm Sunday, I returned to my chapel after an

outstanding weekend retreat with our young people. Jesus had moved strongly while I was preaching, and I was full of joy and power.

After the Sunday service, I took Nancy and the two girls to the car and prepared to head home for a nice dinner. A chicken was in the oven. I remembered my notebook; I had left it inside the chapel. I went back in, and as I walked into the office, I came face to face with the Roman Catholic chaplain. He was furious, red-faced.

"Your people have taken all the palm branches from the altar, and left us nothing," he said rather loudly.

The juices of anger spurted within me. "That's ridiculous. Don't try to blame everything on us! We didn't take your things."

The words flew—out of control. I was in a rage.

As I got into the car, my whole body was trembling. Even in my fury, I was shocked at my weakness as I sat behind the wheel. I finally managed to get the car going, leave the parking lot, and make it home without incident.

The next morning, the chaplain and I sat quietly in our office and talked the matter over sanely. We both knew we had been out of order, and we admitted it. The stand-off passed.

Two days later, a large fever blister rose on my lip. I looked in the mirror, and shook my head. I touched it gingerly. It was a whopper, and sore.

The next day we were sitting in our living room with another couple, and I self-consciously referred to the sore on my mouth. Nancy spoke up. "Do you think your fever blister could have anything to do with your confrontation last Sunday?"

I started to get defensive. But before I could utter a word, a voice inside said, "You'd better believe it did." No one had to tell me the voice was the Lord's.

To the others, I said, "There might be something to that. I'll have to pray about it."

Alone, later, I talked about it to the Lord. "Wow! How dumb can I be? I see it now, Lord. Every time I've gotten angry and sinned, or lost control of myself, the penalty I've had to pay for the emotional upheaval was a fever blister." I sat still for several moments. I realized I couldn't declare that everyone who had a problem with his temper would have fever blisters. But that was what had happened to me. No one could get as angry as I got without experiencing some effects.

I suddenly felt very light and peaceful. A load was gone. I smiled, and then chuckled aloud. "Lord, I thank you. You've healed me of fever blisters and delivered me from Satan's grip on my anger. They're gone!"

It was amazing how the Lord used my health and His Word to bring me to a point of usefulness in those days. The events seemed so minor when compared with the issues of life and death in Vietnam. But they came, one after another.

About once a month, I would develop a nasty cold. My eyes would water and my nose would run. I was miserable, and a sorry sight.

"Lord, heal me of these colds," I would pray as I rushed for the medicine cabinet and tossed down some cold medicine. I sort of liked the drunken, drowsy feeling I got with the pills. Self-indulgence ran quite high. I'd usually take two pills if one was prescribed, figuring I'd get well twice as fast.

The colds continued to come, and I continued to pray for healing. And I also continued to stagger around miserably. After several months at Bragg, I was fed up with this routine. I caught another cold, and I went before the Lord with more sincerity than I had in a long time. I was adamant—perhaps a bit too much so. "Heavenly Father, I know that in your Word you tell me you heal me, and now I trust you to take this sickness from me."

A quiet voice sounded within me. "Are you going to trust me or the medicine cabinet?"

I was actually embarrassed, and spoke very quickly. "Why, *you*, Lord. I trust *you*."

In two hours, the bomb fell. I developed a cold worse than any I'd ever had. I had to go to bed. Tissues flew left and right as I sneezed and wheezed, eyes and nose running. But I avoided the medicine cabinet.

On the third day, it ended. And as I lay in bed, I was sure the cold problem was over. (In the years since, I've had perhaps two one-day bouts with sniffles, but nothing incapacitating, nothing to interfere with God's will for what He had called me to do.)

All I had to do was trust.

I was studying from the letter to the Hebrews in my office one day when I understood more clearly what these little disturbances in my life really amounted to. I was reading about the children of Israel and their problems with entering into God's rest. And I thought about their struggles over the Promised Land as described in the Old Testament. They had had to battle against many enemies even after entering the Promised Land. I saw that my little skirmishes for my "land of promises" were akin to theirs for the Promised Land. I saw that to claim my land I had to step out in faith—in total trust, in total certainty that God was with me and able to do what He had promised. Nothing came without something of a battle. God had never said it would be easy. He'd only said we could enter His rest, and He would do the fighting for us, although we'd have to step out and go forth. As we go, life becomes a bit easier each time, and certainly more joyful.

The practical thing for us to learn from this is that we shouldn't spend all our time asking God to do this, do that.

Rather, we should spend our time seeking His will, seeing what He's doing, and then getting ourselves under His lordship, doing what He's doing. He'll do the rest. We must remember that Jesus said He only did what He saw the Father doing; we, through the Holy Spirit, should be doing only what we see Jesus doing. Then we can rest.

I seemed to be improving on a personal life level, but I was struggling with the ministry. I even had times of struggle over whether the Lord wanted me to stay in the army. Maybe God didn't want me trying to minister to soldiers. Maybe He really wasn't interested in the military after all. At any rate, our chapel program wasn't what I wanted it to be, and I was struggling over it.

I tried to convince people to come to chapel. I called on them in their homes. I met them in their jobs. I even tried to get a choir going. Nothing worked. At the first choir practice we called, the only people to show up were the organist and me.

Our service had been set by the post chaplain for ten A.M., an off-hour by military standards, and no matter what we did, the program merely floundered along. Attendance was meager. No one came to the Bible studies. And the choir idea was our most recent failure.

I stood alone in the chapel one Sunday after a rather dismal service and said aloud, "Lord, I quit! I'm not going to try any more."

The lights flashed on in the darkness of my discouragement, and I thought I could hear soft singing way off in the distance. I burst out laughing. And I laughed steadily for several minutes. I had actually heard singing—the singing of angels. Could this be? I had finally given up and said I would stop trying to run the show myself. And the angels had sung.

"You must be laughing, too, Lord," I said, half-laughing and half-speaking. "Okay. I hear you. I'm just going to *rest*."

From that moment on, week by week, our chapel attendance increased. A Bible study started, and my office was suddenly full of men eager to learn more about God and His Word. Everything came alive.

The frosting came when my commander asked me one day, "Hey, Curry, why don't you start a choir?"

I started to tell him about my efforts, but he broke in. "Get Dwight and his wife to direct it."

He was way ahead of me. All I could do was say, "I'll see what I can do, sir."

Dwight and his wife both held master's degrees in music, but they had never been involved in our program. So I was surprised when they happily agreed to help us. All of a sudden we had an eighteen-voice choir, and they really knew how to sing praises to God.

With hardly a wink of an eye, we had a flourishing chapel. Everything seemed to work like a greased machine.

All I had to do was trust.

And then, there was Nancy. No man ever had a better wife, but believe it or not, I struggled over her, too. I wanted her to enter more fully into the life in the Spirit. I wanted her to experience the miraculous spiritual gifts. I wanted her to speak in tongues. And I pushed her, as so many of us are apt to do with those we love. I was too insistent, and it took some months and a direct word from the Lord before I grew up about it. I finally realized I would have to take Nancy's experience for what it was. After all, I had prayed for her to receive the baptism with the Spirit, and she had claimed it by faith. With an act of the will, I agreed with the Lord that I'd stop worrying about whether she spoke in tongues. I would wait until *His* time. "I give it over to you, Lord," I managed to say. "I quit."

A few days later, I was working in the yard. The Lord spoke to me ever so plainly. "Do you know why Nancy has never spoken in tongues?"

"No, Lord. Why?"

"Because if she had right away, you'd have gone all the way off the deep end."

I winced as I recalled how close I had come to going off the end. Then I grinned. "Father, I thank you for letting Nancy provide a balance for me. I definitely would have gone out of control."

Being a smart woman, as well as a lovely Southern lady, Nancy watched me carefully and perceived the quality of the spiritual things that were happening to me. And she saw the good things happening to others. In fact, she was perceiving more than I was aware of, and it's a good thing I stayed out of the way during those critical stages.

Nancy had never been comfortable with a phrase I had used a lot—"being a fool for Christ." She had equated this with being the town fool, or doing cartwheels in the middle of the street. I had certainly contributed to that impression in the early days of my walk in the Spirit. One night I let myself get back into the middle of things just as we were preparing for bed. Despite having "quit," I was still especially eager for her to be in the swim of things that were unfolding around us, and I sensed the time might be a bit different; I felt the presence of the Lord.

"Nancy," I said a little tentatively, "honey, you're going to have to become a fool for Christ."

The remark hung in the air. And then she coated it with ice. "I don't want to be a fool for anyone."

"But, honey," I said softly as I raised up on one elbow in the bed, "despite some of the things that happened in the past, being a fool for Christ doesn't mean acting wild-eyed or crazy or anything like that. Oh, I know, it may look like that before you step out, but really it results in your being more logical, rational, and capable than ever before—more capable of using what God has given you."

She didn't say anything, but eased softly into bed.

"It just means being free—free in letting the Lord give you everything He wants to," I added quietly, slipping my arm under her head. The ice seemed to have melted as she dropped off to sleep.

I rested; fortunately, I hadn't gotten too pushy.

A short time later, I returned at mid-morning on a hot, muggy day after an all-night prayer meeting with several local people who were preparing for a Nicky Cruz crusade. I was tired and slept most of the day.

At supper, after the girls had gone out to play, I began to talk. I was still tired and a bit edgy, impatient. "Nancy, the Lord has really been putting some things before you lately in relation to speaking in tongues. Even your old friend Worth told you that if you ever were going to speak in tongues, you were going to have to open your mouth and speak out. When are you going to step out?" I looked at her across the table. Had I pushed too far? Had I violated God's rest?

She was looking at her empty plate. "How do you know I haven't already?" She continued to look down, and I couldn't determine the expression on her face.

Five seconds passed. Then I laughed. "Oh, Lord! Nancy, do you mean—? Oh, Lord!" I laughed some more. "Thank you, Lord! Hallelujah! Glory!" I sounded like an old-fashioned Pentecostal.

Without any help from me, my little wife had stood alone with the Lord and told Him she was ready to receive everything He wanted to give her. She had even said she'd be a fool for Him! And He had flooded her with His Spirit so richly and deeply that the well of praise within her had opened wide. She had released what she knew had been there for three years—from the time she first prayed to be baptized with the Holy Spirit. Now it was real.

I was one happy man that night. It had been a *must* for us to be united in Christ, and it was a *plus* for us to be united even beyond that in His Spirit.

All I had to do was trust—which obviously sometimes included stepping out, but not pushing beyond where God was.

As I went forth in my ministry, having "quit," I was sharply aware that I hadn't quit working. Instead, I found myself working longer and harder than ever. And my ministry grew wider, as I saw more of God's plan for the military. But the labor was in the Lord; He did the struggling and fighting.

A giant step forward in this increased, widened work came in the fall of 1970. Needing a break, I had scraped together enough money to attend a charismatic conference in Fort Lauderdale, Florida, my first exposure to large gatherings of people who had had an experience like mine.

One morning I was listening to Bob Mumford, the Bible teacher, talk about television as a means of outreach. He was enthusiastic. "We hope to use it in hospitals, schools, the military. . . ."

Lights flashed in my head. "The military!" The words formed a neon sign in my mind. "These guys are extending themselves to reach the military! They really care, and they're doing something about it." I had completely lost the thread of Mumford's talk by that time.

Then inside I heard the Lord ask a question. "Curry, what's being done in Fayetteville for the charismatic movement to reach the military?"

I whispered barely audibly, "Why, nothing, Lord." No one appeared to hear me.

And that was the end of the exchange. But it was only the beginning of my understanding. I had been given a mission. I was to return to Fort Bragg and get something going in town that would reach our young soldiers for Jesus in a dynamic way. That was the key: *in a dynamic way*. I had been ministering the gospel, but not the *full* gospel, not the full power of the Holy Spirit, not in a widespread way.

I had often been troubled by the fact that I was not where the young soldiers were except during duty hours. Every night, and especially on weekends, there was a massive exit of troops from Fort Bragg. The bulk of them went into Fayetteville. There were wonderful people and good things to do there, but the vast majority of our troops flocked to the center of town, Hay Street, where there was a concentration of drugs, alcohol, and illicit sex, both heterosexual and homosexual. The F.B.I. man responsible for drug abuse in North Carolina had told me that Fayetteville was a center between New York and Miami for dropping drugs. "The word is out," he said. "If you have anything to drop, drop it in Fayetteville."

Yes, I had a mission. And, if I needed any more confirmation of that fact, I got it right away, even before I could leave Fort Lauderdale. The Lord showed me once again that *He* was providing.

The confirmation began on the last night of the conference. Before the meeting, I was sitting with a group around a table in a modest restaurant, eating hamburgers. We were laughing a lot and having a good time. I had ten dollars in my pocket to last me until I got home. That should be no strain if I was careful.

As I finished my second hamburger, the Lord spoke to me. I wasn't ready for it, but there it was. "Curry, I want you to buy everyone's meal." There were four of us.

I looked straight ahead and heard myself saying inside, "Wow, Lord, but—"

"Do it." The voice was gentle, but clear. It was firm.

"Okay, Lord, you know what you're doing," I said a bit childishly under my breath. I wasn't sure my ten dollars would cover the cost, but I stepped out, and collected the checks. "I'll take care of them," I said with a smile that really was only skin deep, and held my breath as the cashier totaled them. I made it. I had three dollars left.

At the last meeting that night, I was sitting back enjoying things when the leader for the evening went to the microphone and said, "Tonight, we're going to take up an offering. But don't put one cent in unless the Lord tells you to do it."

My first thought was that I wouldn't put in anything; I had already given at an earlier meeting. Then I heard a small voice: "Curry, put in all you have."

I shot back instantly, "I rebuke you, devil!"

Silence. Then the small voice: "No, Curry. This is the will of the Lord Jesus for you."

"But Lord," I protested, "I have to travel over a thousand miles tomorrow."

Silence. "Oh, well," I shrugged, "I'll just fast."

The offering plate was handed to me, and I placed the three dollars—all I had—in it. I was a bit apprehensive, but felt I had no other choice.

After the meeting, we were milling around, saying our goodbyes. In the joy of the moment, I forgot I had no money. Just as I was about to walk out the door, a lady came up to me and started to talk about her son. Her words really didn't register or make much sense, it seemed. It was something about her son needing the Lord so desperately. But I couldn't put it all together. Finally, as gently as I could, I excused myself and said I had to get on.

She smiled, and touched my arm, restraining me ever so slightly, and continued to talk for several seconds. I was afraid I'd never get away, and I edged toward the door. Then, she looked up into my eyes. A mother's love was in every cell of her face. "Wait, the Lord told me to give you this."

She placed something in my hand, and stepped immediately away. I looked down. In my hand was a crumpled ten-dollar bill. I looked frantically around the room. She was gone. I didn't even know her name.

I stood still for several seconds. "Thank you, Jesus. I love you, Jesus. Bless that lady, Lord. Thank you for providing our every need."

All I had to do was trust.

Back at Fort Bragg, I sat in my office and wondered how God would ever be able to begin a ministry like the one I had envisioned for Fayetteville. I didn't have any people to help me. But, I thought, what about the group of zealous young soldiers who met in our home for Bible study and prayer each week? Could they be a part of this? What about money? I didn't have anywhere near the amount needed to start something like this. Then I remembered my ten-dollar lesson, and smiled.

In recent months I had met an unusual woman who was actively serving the Lord in the Fayetteville area and even beyond. She was Ruth Stapleton, the wife of a veterinarian, Bob, and, although I didn't realize the significance of it at that time, the sister of a Democratic politician named Jimmy Carter. Bob and Ruth were very kind to me, and I often worked with her on the weekly Bible studies she conducted at Fort Bragg for women. This, in turn, led to broader involvement, through Bible studies and prayer groups, with other citizens. I had no idea of the significance of that, either.

One day, as I grappled with the mission I believed the Lord had given me beyond my regular duties as a chaplain, I was attending one of those study groups in the home of a Fayetteville family. We were having a wonderful time singing, sharing, and praying when one lady spoke up. "I'm here to get healed," she declared. Everyone waited. "I have a vicious headache. I've had these headaches for years." Tears filled her eyes, but she didn't cry.

We were sitting in a sort of irregular circle around the room, and I was close by. I turned to her. "Mary, you know Jesus died for your sins, and He died for your sicknesses, too. Our healing is part of the atonement. He has delivered us from the power of the enemy."

She nodded her head, lowered it, and seemed to close her eyes. I continued to talk. "Let's all of us pray together now, and, Mary, I'll lead you in a simple prayer. The Lord will do the rest."

I paused, and the other people, mostly women, bowed their heads. I continued to look at Mary. "Lord Jesus." She prayed after me. "I give you my life once again. I ask you to forgive me of my sins. I claim your blood upon myself. I command the demon of headaches to get out of my life, in the name of Jesus."

She immediately looked up. She seemed shocked. "It's gone!" Tears spilled onto her cheeks. "It's gone!" Every part of her face shone with the smile spreading out from her lips.

Everyone began to praise the Lord and shout and laugh. Then Mary told us in detail how she had spent more than ten thousand dollars on doctors, pills, and psychiatrists, without any relief. There, in that instant, God had healed her.

After other prayers that morning, Ruth, who had watched Mary's healing intently, came over to me. Her expression was serious. "Curry, Bob and I a long time ago set up a corporation and named it Faith Farms, Inc. We had visions and hopes for how it might be used to serve the Lord, but nothing ever materialized."

A slight smile came to her lips. "But I've been touched by your enthusiasm and your energy—how the Lord is using you. And I think it would be good if we began to work more together to reach this area, the people, for Christ. If you'll put in your energy and zeal, Bob and I will put Faith Farms behind you."

It seemed perfect, ready-made. I had the energy and strength, they had the support. We agreed to seek the Lord's will about it, and to move out.

My work in the chapel at Fort Bragg continued to flourish, and I shared the vision with a few others, praying steadily. One day at noon, a lieutenant, Bob Carmichael, who knew of my mission, came by with a friend to pray. An enlisted man was with me. I closed the door to my office and the four of us got on our knees. We were determined to pray about this wider ministry until God gave us guidance.

After several minutes, Bob looked up and said, "I don't know whether it's the Lord or me, but I keep having this one word come up. It's 'manor.' "

"Manna?" I said.

"No. Manor, m-a-n-o-r."

It didn't make much sense to me, but we all agreed we should not ignore it. "We'll just have to keep an eye out for some mansion or something that God may have for us," I said as we broke up. "If that's the way He wants us to go, we can call it The Manor."

In a few days, Carol Quigg, the wife of a Fayetteville dentist, heard of our plans and said she knew just the house we needed. She took me by to see an old, three-story, wooden house with a large porch running across the front. It was dilapidated and dirty, but we could clean it up. And it was only three blocks from the section we wanted to reach. I would be delighted to have it. It was The Manor; no question about it. We bought it.

A board of directors was established, and God provided a young couple, John and Sandy, to live at the house and manage it. We prayed, and worked, and prayed.

And the doors opened. Immediately alcoholics, drug addicts, the desperate, the lonely, all started filing in. It was overwhelming; we needed people to help us.

Fortunately, the Lord had led Nancy and me to begin a small charismatic fellowship meeting at our home several months earlier. Anywhere from thirty to forty young people—mostly soldiers and their wives, but some civilians—had been squeezing into our relatively small living room each Tuesday night for prayer, study, and a good time. The first thing the Lord had us do was move that meeting to The Manor. That gave us people, and the ministry took off.

Because of my commitments at Fort Bragg, I was able to devote only Tuesday nights and Saturdays to the big house on a regular basis, but I was in constant touch. And other people—clergymen and laymen—came from all over that part of North Carolina to serve.

As far as I knew, no one kept a tally of the numbers who passed through The Manor—which later moved to a newer house a block closer to the downtown area—but young soldiers and civilians came by the hundreds to find Jesus as their Lord and Savior. The Tuesday night meeting especially was wall-to-wall people. The rooms were packed with young and old, white and black, rich and poor, educated and uneducated. There was no distinction between people, no special chairs of honor. It was a tiny taste of Christian community.

One night a soldier wearing a cast on his left leg from the knee down hobbled into the house and sat in a corner. I watched him. He listened intently as we talked about Jesus, and I spoke from the Bible about salvation, about being born again. Near the end of the meeting, he said he wanted to accept Christ as his Savior. We gathered around him, perhaps a hundred of us at that moment, and asked Jesus to enter his life. We then, knowing little about his leg, asked the Lord to heal him.

Three weeks later he returned and asked if he could say

something.

"A little while ago," he began shyly, "I came here and found Jesus. Some of you remember you prayed for my leg. Well, you didn't know it, but I had had a pretty bad motorcycle accident. My leg was all broken up, and the doctors had had to fuse the bone in my ankle and lock it into place."

He stopped and looked around. He was beginning to relax. "The doctors said I'd never be able to walk without a limp. They said I wouldn't have free movement. Well, the week after I was here, I went to the hospital to let the doctor see how my leg was doing. Remember, it had been three weeks since my operation. Well, he took the cast off and had an X-ray taken. When he looked at the picture, he let out a gasp, almost a shout. He called two other doctors in, and they looked at it. And my doc said something like 'how long would you say that ankle has been healing since surgery?' They looked at it again and one said, 'About nine or ten weeks.' The other said, 'About twelve weeks.' My doctor looked at them and really chuckled. 'Three weeks!' he said, all excited. They couldn't believe it."

The soldier stopped talking for a second. Then he lifted his left foot up. It had no cast. "Look at this!" he said, almost yelling. And he moved his foot from side to side and then jumped up and walked around the room without a trace of a limp. He laughed and slapped his leg. Everybody in the room began shouting praises to God.

"What do the doctors think about all this?" I asked when the noise had quieted down.

"They don't believe it," he said. "They say it's impossible for me to do what I'm doing."

And that's the way it went. Week after week, the miracles kept coming. It was an unprecedented time of faith-building for all of us.

But we were so young in the Lord! We made dreadful mistakes, and we fell often into the Christian nemesis—quarreling, gossiping, backbiting. And we often acted when we should have stayed still.

Each of us had ideas about what the ministry should be, and we moved off into some directions that were obviously wrong. But the Lord was good. He brought us back into line at the right times. He blessed us in spite of ourselves. And we learned.

But, more importantly, the gospel went forth to the army and the surrounding community—the gospel with the power of the Spirit. God was touching the military.

The Manor stayed there on Hay Street until recently. Now the ministry has built a new building, called the Manna Church, and it's already overflowing as a local, functioning body of Christ, full of life and power.

As the ministry to the down-and-outers went forward, so did the one to the more prosperous but equally lost members of the community. The Bible study at Fort Bragg prospered. Wives were being blessed, and they were ministering subtly to their husbands. The husbands, officers and enlisted men alike, were then expressing an interest in the Lord.

In one colonel's family, the wife experienced the power of the Holy Spirit in her own life, then her three grown sons entered in, and finally, after some foot dragging, came the colonel. I encountered him one day in an office and, having discussed the subject with him before, asked point-blank if he wanted to receive the baptism with the Holy Spirit. Matter-of-factly, he said, "Yes."

I closed the door and sat down beside him. We joined hands and prayed. "Just speak out in your new prayer language as you feel like it," I said.

"Fine," he said, still matter-of-factly, and he began to speak quietly in tongues. He went on for about fifteen minutes. Then he looked up with a straight face, very matter-of-factly, and said, "This is a very emotional experience, isn't it?"

I almost burst out laughing. I had never seen anyone who appeared to be more unemotional. But for him, *this* was emotion. It was all on the inside.

The wife of another colonel received the baptism with as much exuberance as I'd ever seen in anyone. She went about the post telling about Jesus at command functions, at parties, or anywhere else. Her husband was conservative and quiet. After our Christmas Eve candlelight service, she said aloud to me at the door, with her husband standing beside her, "Curry, do you know what I want him to get for Christmas?"

"No, what?"

"The gift of the Holy Ghost!"

He coughed, quietly, "Ahem. We'd better be getting on."

She got her wish, although it was a few days late.

One friend, an infantry colonel, ran into an extremely bleak time in his career. There at Fort Bragg, at his peak, he was felled with a severe knee injury in an accident at home. I went to see him in the hospital. He lay flat, helpless, with a cast up to his hip. The healing was slow and painful. He feared his command and career were in peril.

We talked quietly and sporadically during that visit, and others later. "I've sure been a proud jerk, Curry," he said, with a weak smile on his rugged face. "I've thought I was accomplishing so much—I was such a great soldier. And, man, I was going to the top!"

He paused. "We're all like that at times, my brother," I said lamely.

"But I was the worst," he said. "I'd want to pat myself on the back and say, 'That's a good job, old boy.' " He laughed ironically. "I really took all the credit I could get. I was a self-sufficient cuss."

We talked like that for several days. And then, in his hospital room, when God was ready, he gave himself totally to Jesus. He was broken. And whoof! The pride was gone. The face was still rugged. He was still a strong soldier. But he was peacefully humble—at rest. He went on to such great faith that I marveled. I could only think of the centurion about whom Jesus spoke, "I have not found so great faith, no, not in Israel" (Matt. 8:10). He gave himself, his family, and his career to Jesus. From a point of nearly losing his command, he recovered and went on to become a general officer, now wearing two stars.

One officer had just moved to our Division Staff when he was flattened by a severe sacroiliac strain similar to the one that had nearly done me in a few months earlier. Christian friends visited him at his home and then asked me to drop by. When I walked in, I hurt for him as I saw him lying motionless but still in agony. His face was creased and strained.

After a few minutes of small talk, with his very pretty wife sitting nearby, he told me about a visit to Fort Bliss in Texas a few days earlier when a friend had offered to pray for him. "Curry," he said, "if God had healed me then and there, He'd have had a disciple. I'd have served him without question."

I liked his honesty, and jumped right in. "But that's not the way it works! You give your life to Jesus. Ask Him in and give Him everything without reservation. Then, if He heals you, fine. But don't try to *deal* with God. Just give Him your life with no strings attached."

He argued back with me. But he listened, too. "I can see that," he said at last. "But it's hard for a guy like me. I'm used to getting something in return."

"Well," I said, "why don't you give it a try the other way? Give without expecting anything in return."

He motioned his wife to the bedside, and clutched her hand.

She smiled beautifully into his face. "Okay," he said. Together they accepted Jesus Christ into their lives—without strings.

The next day he went to the hospital. The doctor had planned to send him to the Walter Reed Army Hospital in Washington. But he examined him and changed his mind. Something had happened. The doctor couldn't explain it, but the officer was practically well.

Not long after that, he went around from person to person at a party telling them what God had done for him. Not everyone listened, of course, but he was giving the glory to the Lord regardless.

And that's the way it went.

I had no explanation that made a lot of sense, but in the midst of all the good activity around me, I was struggling more than ever over whether the Lord wanted me to stay in the army. I prayed almost daily during those weeks about the great conflict within me. Was my place in the chaplaincy?

My expanding ministry was taking me into contact with people I'd never dreamed I'd team up with. More and more, civilian groups called on me to speak and minister. The Full Gospel Business Men's Fellowship, for instance, often called me from widespread places to come and speak. Churches were forever asking me to come. Maybe God wanted me to be a civilian. Maybe he was calling me as a traveling evangelist.

Then the other side of the coin would show. Maybe God wanted me to stay in the army.

For example, I was visiting in the hospital one day with my doctor friend, Gary. We worked a lot together. We stopped at the bedside of a young black soldier, one of Gary's patients. My uniform was hidden under a white hospital gown, so my name and rank were covered. Only my chaplain's cross was visible.

"Have you ever asked Jesus into your life?" I said.

"Yes, when I was in Vietnam."

"What happened?" I asked further, wanting to be sure he knew Jesus and was firm in his decision.

"Well, I was in the 173rd Airborne Brigade."

"What battalion?" I broke in.

"I went down to see my chaplain," he continued, ignoring my question, "and he asked me if I knew Jesus. I told him I didn't, and he asked me to pray with him. Then and there I asked Jesus into my life."

"Praise the Lord," I said. "What battalion were you in?"

"Third," he said.

"Third? Why, that was my battalion! When was it?" I asked excitedly.

"Why, I know you," he said as his eyes lighted. "*You* were the chaplain!"

I practically shouted, "Thank you, Jesus!" Several patients turned to look at us. We talked excitedly for several more minutes, and I was as happy as I'd been in months. The Father had done me a great favor. I had often wondered what had happened to those four hundred men who had made decisions for Jesus. Now here was one who had testified of his faith in Christ even before he recognized me. This really confirmed Philippians 1:6 to me: ". . . he which hath begun a good work in you will perform it until the day of Jesus Christ." Truly the Holy Spirit followed up people who made sincere decisions in Him. I had, under the circumstances, been unable to follow up with spiritual guidance to many of the men I had prayed with. But *He* had done it!

It was this sort of thing that caused me to vacillate so. I wrestled hard. I fervently wanted God's will, but what *was* it? Why didn't I have peace in the midst of so much blessing?

It was easy in those days for a Spirit-filled Christian to think he was the only one interested in spreading the Word in the army. That was far from the case. God was moving in many people's lives, and they weren't standing still.

Ralph E. Haines, Jr. was a prime example. He wasn't just an ordinary soldier, and he wasn't a chaplain, either. He was a four-star general and, more than that, the Continental Army Commander, which meant he was the commander of all forces based in the continental United States. He reported to the Chief of Staff.

I had heard a bit about his experience with God.

In the spring of 1972 he made a special trip to Fort Bragg. It was something he was doing to all the posts. We got word that he was coming and wanted to meet with all commanders, sergeants major, and chaplains. It was not a command performance, we were told, but nobody believed that, not when you were dealing with the continental commander. We knew that, among other things, he was going to talk about religious and moral responsibilities of command. I really didn't know what to expect, but I dropped him a note to let him know I was in his corner. He wrote back: "Hey, thanks. I appreciate it. I'll be down there."

It was early afternoon, a sunny spring day. I walked into the main post chapel and it was jam-packed with close to five hundred men. I took a seat about a third of the way in from the rear. The old chapel was pretty. I looked up at the big chandelier in the center of the high ceiling, then down to the high, crow's-nest pulpit. Almost everything was painted white.

Suddenly a sound of boots on the wooden floor came from the doorway at the rear. Someone said, "Attention," and everyone rose. There was Haines, striding briskly beside the corps commander. Everyone was dressed in fatigues. Haines went directly to the front and turned to face the men. I was glad he didn't use the pulpit.

Haines was a good-looking man, I noticed, serious-faced but

not unfriendly. His face was very tan, and his brown hair neatly combed. He was a man of authority.

He launched right into his talk without formality. "Gentlemen, I thank you for turning out this afternoon." His voice was penetrating, but not especially loud. "I want to talk to you for a few minutes about command responsibility and some of the things we run into as commanders. And I want to share with you some thoughts and experiences I've had. I believe that is part of my responsibility."

He was speaking without notes, and his words seemed to come easily. I was curious, and just a bit tense, I noticed.

"I feel, as a commander, a strong sense of responsibility for the whole man serving under me. I feel a responsibility for the spiritual and moral well-being of the men and women, as well as for their mental and physical well-being. I believe that many of the problems we are facing—racial, drug, dissension, and such—are basically moral and spiritual in nature. And I believe that we, as commanders, must understand this. This is not something just for the chaplains. It's the commander's responsibility."

Then, for the next few minutes, this unusual, dignified, slightly graying man spoke intimately about his personal experience. The room was absolutely quiet, except for a muffled cough now and then. It took a minute or two for me to realize that he was going to tell about his baptism with the Holy Spirit. "Praise the Lord; he's got courage," I said under my breath.

He told how he, as a recognized Christian, had been invited to Buffalo to speak at a regional meeting of the Full Gospel Business Men's Fellowship. He hadn't known the group, he said, but it was conducting a military breakfast along with its other meetings, so he had accepted.

Arriving the night before he was to speak, he attended the dinner meeting and was soon involved in a manner of worship he was unaccustomed to, as a staunch Episcopalian. Most of the five or six hundred people there seemed to pray aloud, sing with gusto, and laugh a lot. Then the main speaker talked inspiringly on how the power of the Holy Spirit was being experienced in current times just as it had been in the early church. He concluded with a prayer in which everyone was asked to join. Several minutes of praise in song and prayer followed.

"Suddenly," the general said, with the slightest smile on his face, "I felt myself filled with such a surge of love and joy that, even now, I am at a loss for words to describe it. As I entered more and more into that deep moment of worship, I experienced a real bathing in the Holy Spirit. I was baptized afresh to a new, closer walk with the Lord."

Softening ever so slightly, he told how that, during the prayer, he began to hear a strange language. Then he realized it was his voice. He—a four-star general in full uniform—was speaking in tongues in the middle of that great crowd.

He paused. "I was profoundly moved," he said, "and more than a little bit unnerved." He smiled more broadly then and told how, before long, he found himself a changed man. "I was a better man, a better husband, a better officer," he said emphatically.

Haines spoke for several more minutes, encouraging those five hundred men at Fort Bragg to face up to what he considered to be this critical part of command responsibility. He urged them not only to seek God for themselves, but also to be concerned about this dimension of their people's lives.

I looked around to see what was happening in the audience. Everything was quiet, but tension showed on many faces. I could almost feel the people struggling and tightening. Most of them were not used to that sort of talk, not even in a chapel. And, obviously, many of them didn't like it.

In a moment, the general was finished. He had spoken for

almost an hour. A sergeant major near the front, clearly a Christian, got to his feet and said rather loudly, "Praise the Lord!" That ended the meeting, and we were dismissed.

"Hello, Curry."

I looked around. It was a colonel I had known for some time.

"Curry," he said, shaking his head from side to side, "do you know what has happened here? I really appreciate General Haines—you know, the courage and freedom he showed in doing this."

I nodded without saying anything.

"But, do you know, something very special and very personal happened to me. There's no reason you'd know it, but I've been through a very bad time—the worst time in my career." He began to weep very quietly. "I had to relieve a battalion commander for alcoholism, and it was a battle, a bad scene. I never got into anything so ugly in all my life. It's still ugly."

"I can understand," I said softly, not wanting to divert him.

"Well, I've really been in a depression, and going through a lot of guilt stuff, and all that. It may be hard to understand, but it's been real hell. But I hear Haines, and the way he sees command, and the way he trusts God, and all of a sudden the whole thing is lifted. All the guilt just went away."

He was near the point of sobbing, his emotions strained, but he blurted out, "All I can say is praise the Lord!"

I liked that. Here was a full colonel living in a kind of hell, really suffering, and this general, not the chaplain, ministered to him. The Holy Spirit was able to touch him.

Ralph Haines went to every post in his command, laying his experience and his recommendations on the line. Lives were touched. Many were offended as they felt he was putting religious pressure on them, which they believed was improper and perhaps unconstitutional. But Haines was instrumental in spreading the gospel in many parts of the army.

He did eventually run into open criticism, and it probably contributed to his being forced to take early retirement, although the Pentagon and the White House firmly denied it. Many had expected him to become Chief of Staff, but, in his words, he settled for being "a private in the army of the Lord."

9

REST

I still could not decide what I should do with my life. I knew the time was coming, and quickly, when I would be forced to make some important decisions. I had been told, for instance, that very soon I would be selected to attend the Chaplains Career School at Fort Hamilton in Brooklyn, New York. It was a good step, from a career point of view, but I was troubled that it could remove me from active ministry for a year and would tend to seal me into the chaplaincy. I was still having trouble accepting the idea that God had called me to a life as an army chaplain.

Then my orders for Fort Hamilton arrived, and I was half sick. I had enjoyed the years of whirlwind ministry; things had happened everywhere I'd been. Surely, God didn't want to bench me. Finally I had to do something. So I prayed. I didn't believe fleeces were the way, so I sought God's mind, and asked Him to lead me by His Spirit as His son. I knew the sons of God were led by His Spirit (Rom. 8:14).

After many painful hours of praying, I could honestly say I was willing to stay in or get out of the army. But I was in total confusion. "Lord, just lead me," I pleaded.

With orders in hand, I made a covenant with the Lord in March. I agreed to wait until the Fourth of July to make my final decision, asking Him to make the path clear by then.

During those days, I read a book by Bob Mumford, *Take Another Look at Guidance.* One night I came across three indicators he felt should be in accord before one made a decision: the Word, the inner peace given by the Holy Spirit, and the circumstances. I put the book in my lap and stared into space. "I've only got one of those working in me right now," I said semi-audibly. "And that's the peace. I've got the peace of the Spirit when I think about leaving the army."

I closed my eyes and thought a few moments. I began slowly to feel that the Lord was leading me out, even though I could see only one of those indicators.

Several days passed, and my thoughts continued in the same vein. I was in my office alone when certainty seemed to fall. I jumped up from behind my desk. "All right, Lord. I'm going to get out of the army!"

That must have been sheer impulse, however, and even I had to admit it. For there had been no leading from the *Word,* and there were no *circumstances* for me to move into. I was making decisions on the basis of only one of the three indicators.

In those days, I began to do even more speaking and sharing of my experiences in church renewals, especially in my own Presbyterian denomination. As the tempo increased, I thought that perhaps there was something for me there—maybe those were the circumstances. But they were very shaky, if they existed at all.

One weekend, I was in Charlotte, North Carolina, when the command God had given to Abraham crossed my mind: "Get thee out of thy country, and from thy kindred, and from thy father's house. . . ." (Gen. 12:1). I paraphrased this to "go out of the land of your fathers" and thought perhaps this was referring to the army. After all, the army was in a sense the "land of my fathers"—my father and my father-in-law. Could it be? I mulled it over. Maybe this was something from the *Word*; and I still had *peace in my heart*.

With seemingly two of the three indicators in hand, I stepped forth boldly and declared that I was going to leave the army. I even called the Chaplain Personnel Office in Washington to announce my intentions. What more could the Lord want? I was laying my career—and that was my life—on the line. I would step out and go where He led.

Many friends began to pray with me about my situation, and at last I thought I could see some *circumstances* opening up. The Manor in Fayetteville, still flourishing, needed a full-time, salaried minister, and I was approached by the members of the board to take on that job. Reserving the right not to make a final decision until the Fourth of July, I temporarily agreed that if the Lord seemed to be leading, I would take it.

Meanwhile, Jerry Daley, a graduate of the Air Force Academy and Fuller Seminary, popped into our lives through some of the Fayetteville people. They had met Jerry and called him east for an interview about the Manor ministry. He and I prayed and talked at length about the work. The more we talked, the more excited he became. He saw great potential there. Strangely, the more excited he became, the more my enthusiasm waned. I could see the inner peace of the Spirit flickering. In a short time, I swung all the way over to the conviction that I had done all God wanted me to do at the Manor. I loved the people. We had been through dramatic times together. But those times had passed, for me.

The light of the inner peace flickered out, and with it went the circumstances.

One morning, I was getting dressed in my bedroom. Standing in front of the mirror, I looked at myself clearly and carefully. I looked at my face. I looked at my frame—and then back into my face.

I heard no voice, but I knew the thoughts walking carefully and unhastily through my mind at that moment were valid. They were safe to heed. "I was born and raised in the army environment . . . I have valuable experience as an infantryman . . . I was able to go to seminary and remain in the army . . . I ministered and survived in war . . . My ministry bore fruit . . . I liked—loved—the army. . . ."

After several moments of virtual blankness, the thoughts resumed. By this time, I knew they were from the Lord. "Doesn't it make sense that you should stay where you are?" they concluded.

In the mirror, I saw I was nodding my head. "Yes, Lord," my lips said, and I recalled the advice I had more than once given to someone searching for guidance: "Do what seems right, and trust God." I nodded my head again.

That was it. Everything fit into place. I had the *inner peace,* and as I stood before the mirror I suddenly had the *Word*—"Let every man abide in the same calling wherein he was called" (1 Cor. 7:20). Of course, the *circumstances* were there; they always had been. I had a very definite place and role in the army. There were hundreds, thousands, of people who were hungry for Christ and the power of the Holy Spirit. God appeared to have a plan for the military; it appeared He loved soldiers, too.

"Okay, Lord," I said into the mirror, "it's not the Fourth of July yet, and I'll keep my covenant, but I'm ready to go to that school and stick with it until you show me something else."

Fort Hamilton was a shock. Nancy and I and our two girls had been used to the beautiful, open countryside of North Carolina, and suddenly we were plopped into Brooklyn—in the middle of the New York metropolitan area, population twenty million. The cars, the buildings, the pollution, the filth in the streets, the crime, the masses of people—these were all beyond our imaginations. I knew that we were going to have to make tremendous adjustments.

I learned quickly that city people were accustomed to being nasty to one another. The day we were to move into our tiny, two-bedroom apartment on the fourth floor of a six-floor building, the elevator broke down. It was a brutally hot July day. I was out taking care of some business when Nancy was confronted by our movers. She opened the door and four burly men marched in. They walked around and around her, huffing and puffing angrily.

"Do you know the elevator is out?" one said. "We can't move nobody when the elevator is out! Did you call the building superintendent? We're going to call the boss!"

The sentences ran together. Nancy hadn't said a word. Before she could open her mouth, the men stalked out.

I arrived as they left, and Nancy told me what had happened. We prayed on the spot, asking God to do something. The movers could walk out for a week as far as we knew, and we desperately needed to act right then. We had no place else to go.

Thirty minutes later they were back. "We're going to move you up and over," one said.

"What do you mean?" I asked.

"Well, we decided to go to the elevator in the next stairwell. That'll get us to the top floor. Then we go up one flight of stairs to the roof and across to your stairwell and down three flights to your floor."

It sounded very complicated to me, but if that's what would get our things moved in, I was all for it.

Several hours later, when much of the move had been laboriously accomplished, the military transportation representative came by. He watched the movers carrying our furniture and turned to me, shaking his head. They were sweating and puffing. "Chaplain, I've been in this business twenty years, and I've never seen a moving company do for anyone what these people are doing for you!"

"It's the Lord," I said innocently.

"It's *some*thing," he said. "These people just don't do these things."

Once again, I knew the Lord was taking care of us. True, our life in that strange environment was full of little difficulties and irritations, but we knew we were being directed.

I began my studies for a master's degree in counseling, taking courses at Long Island University. And I eventually got a chance to keep my hand in the ministry when I rather surprisingly got a preaching assignment at a Presbyterian church in Queens. I was asked to preach for a month, but ended up staying the whole year. I chafed a bit under what I considered to be a dull, monotonous life after all the excitement of North Carolina. But the Lord very gently laid on me a powerful question. "Curry, how do you think Paul felt when he was in jail?"

Naturally, I winced, and once more knew I had to rest. Like Paul, I had to learn to be content no matter what the conditions were.

There were times of excitement, however, but not all of it pleasant. Probably the most difficult time came a few weeks after I began ministering in the church in Queens. It started one Saturday when two girls from the youth group showed up at the church and wanted to talk about the baptism with the Holy Spirit. I gladly told them about it, from the Scripture and from my own life, and led them into the experience.

One week later, I was in the middle of a hot controversy. The youngsters had naturally told their parents, and word of their experience spread like wildfire. Two men in the church confronted me, and I privately explained my position. But that didn't settle the matter; the whole congregation was in an uproar. I hadn't run into that sort of thing before. My first reaction was to think of repentance. I was almost sorry I had helped those two kids come into the blessing of God.

Then came one of those little conversations with the Lord. "Did you do this in obedience to me?" He asked as I was alone one night.

"Yes, Lord, I did."

"Then you know you don't have to defend this or me."

I wasn't happy about that. I wanted to get up in the pulpit Sunday morning and bring out all the artillery in my defense, but the Lord said: "No, Curry, don't speak one word publicly in your own behalf. Continue to preach the gospel, and love those who are troubled."

"But . . . but . . . but. . . ."

It was a hard lesson. And it was the second time in recent weeks that the Lord had spoken to me about it. The first time came during the Chaplains Career Course, when we spent hours talking in small group sessions. On two or three occasions, I became upset with some of the men I felt didn't take the Bible as seriously as I did, or who were skeptical about the charismatic renewal. It was so bad that one of the chaplains spoke to me: "Curry, I've noticed that the only time you really get upset is when you think someone is criticizing your ministry or the things you stand for."

I knew he was right, for I heard the Lord quietly say: "Curry, stop defending me."

This, coupled with the controversy at the church, showed me that if I really believed what I was doing was right and from God, I didn't need to defend it.

When Sunday morning came after the blow-up over the two youngsters at the church, I took the pulpit and preached on salvation through Christ as it applies both eternally and in this life. I ignored the controversy. It didn't go away, but I dealt with it one person at a time as the occasion warranted, and refused to fight over it. It was difficult, but over the next four months I felt the ice melt. When I finally left the church, I knew all of us were one in Christ, in spite of our differences over the work of the Holy Spirit. I had taken another step in allowing God to do battle for His people.

Near the end of our year at Fort Hamilton, we chaplains were taken to Camp Pickett in Virginia, a part of Fort Lee, for a two-week exercise to improve our staff work for high levels. Each morning I got up at six o'clock to jog. It was invigorating and inspiring to run through the countryside and breathe the fresh air of the gently rolling Virginia hills.

One morning I set out and decided to run to a lake I'd heard about. I wasn't sure of the distance, but figured I could handle it. It turned out to be two miles, and I needed a rest after I got there. I walked to the shore line and then out onto an old dock. I sat and enjoyed the quiet beauty of the lake. There were no sounds of man, no intrusions of society. A fish jumped, a frog croaked, bugs skipped across the water. The air was full of lively spring odors.

"Lord," I said aloud, "I want you to know that I love you from the depth of my innermost being. I want you to know that."

I felt extremely close to God at that moment. I paused and then burst ahead. "Heavenly Father, I want to make a deal with you. I promise that I will serve you wherever you call me. I'll go to any job or calling that you send my way as an army chaplain. I only ask in return that you always give me a ministry wherever I go."

It was a deal, and I felt very good about it. I didn't give a second thought to the fact I hadn't heard God say anything in return. I was certain He was pleased. I had totally surrendered to the Lord, and was truly willing to serve Him in the army. I asked only one small thing—to have a ministry.

I rose from the dock and ran almost effortlessly the two miles back to my quarters. I was at the beginning of a new surge in my ministry.

Each night while we were at Camp Pickett, another chaplain and I led a prayer and praise service in the chapel. It was small, drawing eight to ten men from the base. One night a young fellow called Chuck showed up. He had a can of beer in his pocket and he thought it was a real joke to have brought it into the church. We just let him talk.

As the week went on, he became more disruptive, talking and laughing at the wrong times, and generally making a nuisance of himself. But one night, I pressed him on turning to Christ as his Savior. I knew he was there for a reason, whether he knew it or not. After considerable discussion, he did pray with us and asked Jesus into his life. At first he seemed fine, but later in the meeting he jumped up and ran out. We let him go, wondering if he'd ever come back.

The next night he was there again. Several of us began to pray, and two or three of the men reached over and put their hands on him. Without warning, he began to fall out of his seat. I edged forward and caught him, easing him gently to the floor. He remained unconscious, or seemingly so, for five minutes as we continued to pray for him.

When he came to, we sat around and talked for quite a while. Soon he began talking freely about a childhood friend named Sham. When he was younger, his closest friend was Sham.

"One day we were out playing, just the two of us, near a river," Chuck said softly, his eyes occasionally staring into the distance. "Sham got this idea that we should go out into the river, jumping from rock to rock. I was scared and didn't want to do it, but Sham was insistent. He could be real persistent.

We got quite a ways from shore, and all of a sudden I saw Sham slip. He waved his arms, trying to get his balance, but he fell into the water."

Chuck paused, and looked from face to face. Then he continued. "He began to cry for help, but I thought he was just kidding. I thought he could swim fairly well and was sure he was just acting out. By the time I knew he was serious, it was too late. He went under. He died right there."

He stopped, and very quietly repeated, "He died right there."

He went on to describe the guilt he'd felt over Sham's death. He felt he had let his good friend die.

After a few minutes we began to pray again, and Chuck once again asked Jesus to take over his life. But without warning, he jumped up and ran out, just as on the previous night. This time, I asked two of the guys to go with him and try to help him. We kept on singing and praying. But off in the distance I heard strange sounds. I was sure I heard someone screaming at the top of his voice.

It was nearly midnight when the meeting ended, and I went to Chuck's barracks to look for him. He wasn't there, but as I went out front, he and the two other fellows walked up.

"Chuck," I said enthusiastically, "how are you?"

He was wild-eyed and confused. "Sham," he said. "I saw Sham burning in the fire." Tears covered his face. "Sham is burning."

"Chuck," I said gently, "let's go talk. Let's go talk in my office."

I finally persuaded him to come with me, and the two others joined us as we walked to the old building where we'd been assigned work areas.

"Have a seat, Chuck," I said once we were inside. "Now I want to tell you what's going on." The others sat quietly on each side of us. "I really feel that the devil has hold of you. I need every bit of cooperation you can give me. I want you to will with everything in you that the demon be cast out. Do you understand that? And are you willing?"

"Yes," he said evenly, looking straight ahead.

As I led him, Chuck prayed with relative ease. I rebuked the devil and commanded him to name himself, constantly claiming the blood of Christ. Chuck also repeated "the blood of Jesus" over and over. But nothing seemed to happen.

Finally, I stopped and, to myself, called on the Lord for wisdom or knowledge as to how to proceed. He seemed to speak to me: "Have Chuck look at you."

I spoke aloud. "Chuck, I want you to look at me." He looked up and my eyes met his. I looked into the face of a devil. Chuck's face was twisted and contorted, his eyes glazed and wild. His nostrils were contracting and expanding like those of a cornered wild animal.

"Chuck," I said evenly but firmly, "I want you to say, 'Jesus is my Lord.' "

He couldn't say anything. He opened his mouth and grunted, but nothing coherent came out. Finally, with great difficulty, he asked Jesus to help him and twenty minutes later gasped, "Jesus is my Lord." It was completely unnatural.

I knew we hadn't broken through. So I fixed my eyes on his and spoke strongly, "Demon, I command you to name yourself and come out of him, in the name of Jesus."

Still nothing. I repeated the command. "Demon, name yourself and come out of him."

Chuck gasped. I listened closely. "Sh . . . sh . . . sha . . ."

"Name yourself," I said again.

Chuck strained with all his might. The veins stood out on his neck. "Sh-sh-sh-a-a-am," he blurted out.

It was clear. "Sham," I said forcefully, "you demon, in the name of Jesus, come out of him." I paused, and then said it again. Chuck's face was so tight I thought it would burst. He strained and, following me, himself rebuked the demon.

Suddenly he was free. His face eased. He virtually slumped in the chair, drained. But he was okay, relaxed. He soon smiled, and his eyes were clear.

All of us together prayed to see if other demons were present, but he was free. We discussed the whole matter and realized what had happened. Chuck had taken on a tremendous burden of guilt after Sham's death. This had made him vulnerable to demonic deception and then possession, and the demon had taken the name of his childhood friend to keep him deceived.

Later that night, I knew the Lord had given me a big lesson in my walk with Him. I had been awkward and inexperienced, but I felt I had stepped into a new dimension in my ministry.

The year at the Chaplains Career School ended, and I was assigned to Kitzingen, Germany. I was to "leave the land of my fathers." Nancy and I were delighted about our orders for Germany. I had been there as a child right after World War II when my father was part of the postwar occupation force. I had returned for a short term as a West Point cadet, and now we were going again. I knew only that I would work in the Third Infantry Division.

A short time later, my orders were modified to send me to Wurzburg, not far from Kitzingen. I could feel rebellion rising in my throat as I read the orders. Kitzingen was a perfect duty assignment with troops—my kind of work. Why was I being sent down the road to a headquarters?

It took only seconds for me to recognize the thought easing gently into my mind. It was the Lord's. "Am I running the show, or do you want to try?"

I winced, but managed to smile. "Okay, Lord, I'll say no more."

Just before departing, Nancy and I squeezed in a vacation trip that gave us two exciting, but relaxing weeks that convinced me we were ready for new vineyards. First there was the Family Life Conference sponsored by the Presbyterian Church at Montreat, North Carolina; then a beautiful trip through North and South Carolina that included a stop at the Manor in Fayetteville, where we were delighted to see the blessings of God upon His people. I once again encountered folks, young and old, whom Jesus had allowed me to touch in His name. The gospel was working.

Furthermore, at the last moment before our departure for Germany, an old friend and classmate, Jim Sorenson, called from Columbus, Ohio, asking me to come to appear on a television show with him. It would be tight, but it seemed important, and the airline schedules fit perfectly.

Jim and I drove from Columbus to Akron for the TV taping. It was the *Good News* show sponsored by the Full Gospel Business Men's Fellowship, and we were to be interviewed by Demos Shakarian, the organization's founder. Demos met us in the studio, and we hadn't been there five minutes when he asked if I knew Bob Crick.

"Know him?" I shouted. "Why, he's the one who led me into the whole experience of the baptism with the Holy Spirit!"

"Well, he's here right now for a taping," Demos laughed.

It was a joyful reunion. I knew God was blessing me in an unusual way. Something was up.

Then, with only minutes to spare, Jim put me on a plane bound for Washington, where I would connect for New Jersey, and then on to Europe.

I settled in my window seat aboard the twin-engine jet. It was an especially beautiful day. The jet rose up above the clouds, and the sun dipped off on the horizon. The sky was a brilliant red, and the glory of God seemed to be declared by every cloud.

Unexpectedly, a very peaceful feeling settled over me. I was stirred by the beauty around me, but totally restful inside. I recognized the presence of the Lord, and knew somehow that the moment might be the most significant of my life.

I began to talk to Him inside. The thoughts were overwhelmingly peaceful and right. "Lord," I said, "I've been struggling for a long time. I made a *deal* with you just a few weeks ago. It was a deal, almost like a scheme, and yet you blessed me. But I know I've been struggling because of it."

I was oblivious to all around me. "Now, my dear heavenly Father, I want to change that deal. I want to give you my life. This time I give it with no deals and no strings attached. I love you, Jesus, and I give everything. Use me however you will—with a ministry or without a ministry. I am yours unreservedly."

I touched my face. It was wet with tears, and I kept it turned toward the window so the other passengers wouldn't see me.

I knew that for the first time in my life I had quit struggling. I had been able to accept God's will for my life no matter what. And I had not planned this experience. I had not anticipated it. God had done it. He had let me look back—back to all my friends and experiences—and now was moving me forward.

New realizations flooded me as I looked into the darkening blue sky. I had been a Christian for twenty-two years, but I had never really given myself to the Lord entirely. I had always wanted to have my little say in any situation. That's why I had made my deal before. I was saying, "Lord, I'll serve you *if*—" when I should have been saying, "I'll serve you no matter what." Jesus died for me without reservation. I had to serve Him without reservation—without covetousness. This did not invalidate my previous experience. I had been born again and baptized with the Holy Spirit. I had ministered in the power of the Spirit. But my experience had been far from full.

"Yes, Lord." I was nodding my head as the revelations flowed into me. The Bible's words of rest and refreshing were so real. The letter to the Hebrews in itself was full of such instruction, especially in chapter four. I could almost see the words. "Let us therefore fear, lest, a promise being left us of entering into his rest, any of you should seem to come short of it" (vs. 1). And again, "There remaineth therefore a rest to the people of God" (vs. 9).

I knew I had entered into that rest, at least far more than I ever had before. Completion and perfection were still a long way off, but I had entered in. And, in doing so, I had destroyed the place I had unwittingly given Satan in my life. As long as I had rebelled in even the smallest way, I had refused God full reign in my life, and that had provided a platform—at least a small one—for the devil. Now that platform had hopefully been smashed.

Looking out the window, I was amazed at how simple and logical this seemed and yet how long it had taken for me to arrive at this point. "Father," I said, "I don't see how or why you've blessed my ministry in the past, but you have, and I thank you. I hope I'm a better vessel now."

I felt ready for Germany.

10

THE CHURCH

I stood in the middle of the chapel. It was empty—empty and big and quiet, restful. No sounds penetrated the high walls. I rubbed my hand over the polished dark trim of the white pews and walked slowly toward the altar. We had just arrived in Wurzburg, and this was where I'd work. I stepped softly, sweeping my eyes across the wide, white-ceilinged sanctuary. "It will hold at least four hundred," I thought. It was the post's community chapel, the largest of four churches there. The stained-glass windows in the back gave it an age and stateliness that belied its relatively short history.

I walked across to the pulpit and stepped up. It was a fine pulpit. I could see every pew. Placing a hand on each side of the dark-brown lectern, I closed my eyes and became totally quiet. I couldn't even hear my breathing. After fifteen seconds, I spoke aloud.

"Lord, I just want to let you know that this is your pulpit." I paused and bowed my head ever so slightly. The silence was deep. "God, it's yours, and I ask you to do with it whatever pleases you. I'm just here to speak for you, to work for you—to do whatever you want."

I stood in the pulpit for fully three minutes. It was a worshipful spot, holy. "This will be very good," I said, stepping down. I walked back out into the rain.

It was raining when we arrived the day before, and it continued. Germany seemed to be a place of rain. We had landed in Frankfurt on July 19, 1973, and were driven sixty miles east to Wurzburg, a city of one hundred thousand people, eight thousand of them Americans. Nancy and I were exhausted, but the two girls were full of life. We struggled our way through the first day, jet lag and all, and were immediately impressed with the fact that so many of the people we were running into seemed to talk a lot about Jesus. The people around the chapel offices, our new acquaintances, acted like people who loved the Lord. "This is heaven," I thought.

I was the assistant division chaplain for the Third Infantry Division and the pastor of the main chapel. It took about two days for me to realize fully that the chapel program was in a shambles, but understandably so. The previous workers had all been rotated out about the same time as the previous chaplain, and we were left without a choir, an usher committee, a Bible study, or a men's group. The women's group was about the only one continuing into the summer and even that was soon threatened when the leader's husband was transferred back to the states. Furthermore, some of the commitment to Christ I had initially observed might be only skin deep. That was the most serious discovery of all.

My new job and the sad condition of the chapel work soon had me dragging. No matter how many hours I put in during those first few days, I could see no progress. One night I sat in my office in front of a pile of papers on my desk. My head pounded with frustration. I finally slipped my pencil onto the desk, leaned back in the chair, and spoke out in exasperation. "Lord, I just can't do it!"

I stopped, and seemed to sense the word "Good."

Then I spoke on. "As I have done in the past, I give all of this to you."

It was Fort Bragg all over again. I had to come to the point of resting. God would have to raise up the workers to do the tasks.

I had been there eight days. It was my second Sunday, and my first participation in the regular chapel service. The sanctuary was only one-third filled, but I didn't mind. I stepped up into the pulpit and began to preach on one of my favorite themes, "Being a Fool for Christ."

"Everybody's somebody's fool," I said. "Consider the guy carrying a sign up and down in front of a building. On the front it says, 'I'm a fool for Christ.' Everybody looks at it, and some laugh, but as they go by, they turn and look at the other side, which says, 'Who's fool are you?' "

I kept it short and straightforward. My Vietnam days had aimed me toward directness, and I stayed that way for the most part.

"To be God's fool," I said, "means that you have to be willing to let go of the rational, the logical, the traditional, if necessary, and to take a leap of faith to God. It doesn't mean you then become the village idiot. It means you become so sensitive and sold out to Christ and to His voice that you can respond to Him, and in so doing you, God's fool, start becoming a whole person. You find you are becoming such a rational, logical, total person that your personality starts to extend into a fullness and a completeness that it never knew without Christ. But you've got to be willing to be a fool for Christ. You've got to be sold out to Him. Halfway is not good enough."

The reaction was strong, and immediate. Many of the people apparently were used to being entertained. But the Lord had persuaded me to refrain from the dramatic, from the emotional, and to speak the Word—even blandly—and let it do its work. It seemed to create a bit of discomfort that morning.

The following Sunday I planned to preach on "Being a Child of the King." We brought in a couple of the young people with guitars to sing and to lead us in song, and the atmosphere took on a different tone from the standard-brand chapel service of those days. There was a trace of spontaneity and freedom. One young soldier even unexpectedly testified about his acceptance of Christ and immediate deliverance from a severe drug habit. One of the guitar-playing youths blurted out enthusiastically, "Praise the Lord!" It was a change. Simultaneously with the freedom came a touch of nervousness in the congregation. I could feel it.

I went forward to receive the offering plates from the ushers and was on my way to place them on the altar when I heard a voice as clear as any I'd heard. It surprised me.

"Curry, you know if you keep on messing around like this, they're going to throw you out of here."

It was amazing; the voice was so real. But I was alone in front of the altar. For a second I was frightened. Then I smiled. That was not the Lord's voice. I spoke directly into the altar: "Praise the Lord! This is it! I must go on!" The battleground extended even to the front of God's altar.

I mounted the pulpit and spoke evenly and simply: "Are you a child of the King? . . ."

It was soon obvious that much of the real spiritual life among the Americans at Wurzburg was in the young soldiers and their wives. They were the ones who were outspokenly excited about Jesus. And much of their activity centered on three coffeehouses that had opened sometime earlier with a lot of help from a chaplain who had preceded me and from Youth With A Mission. It was obviously a good, dynamic work that had fallen right into step with the coffeehouse movement of those days. And I fully identified with it. Most of the young people had received the baptism with the Holy Spirit and were excited about the charismatic renewal.

Several couples and many single soldiers practically lived in those places. They talked about Jesus, read the Scriptures, sang, prayed, and did whatever else they thought the Lord wanted them to do. Most, if not all, of them had been on drugs. Now they were one hundred per cent for Jesus, and they witnessed continually to those around them. In essence, they formed a church, and were closely identified with one another; they loved and supported each other. And their zeal caused their number to multiply.

It was soon apparent that this contributed to a gap in the American Christian community. The older people were involved only in Sunday worship, and the young people were for the most part off by themselves.

Because of my identification with them at least in the charismatic renewal, some of the young people at the coffee houses started coming to Sunday chapel services. They'd sit down front and really join in the worship. I could hear them softly praying in tongues, for instance, and I could sense this troubled some of the choir members. And they'd raise their hands occasionally, and now and then let slip an audible "Praise the Lord." As I expected, this caused some tension. But surprisingly, as I just let it happen, saying nothing, the older, more traditional people finally settled back and relaxed, and the younger members of the congregation continued to increase. The gap was narrowing.

We soon began what we called a Jesus Rally every Thursday night at the chapel, primarily for the young people, the fifteen to thirty who were the most active in the charismatic renewal. It was a rowdy meeting, with everyone raising his hands and many screaming in tongues at the top of their voices. It was so rowdy, in fact, that I considered intervening. But the Lord kept assuring me that it was all right for the time being to let the youngsters express themselves, to vocalize their love for the Lord, even if they did seem a bit out of order. Indeed, I was not edified by the meetings; they weren't sweet, at least to me. But they were fun and free and, despite my anxiety, the Lord seemed to say, "Leave it alone for now, Curry."

God prospered the meetings. Steadily they grew, and more and more people were blessed.

And the Lord began to move, little by little, on the more traditional element in our community.

One night in the officers' club, Nancy and I met Lieutenant Colonel R.J. Wooten and his wife, Mary Ann. As we talked, I learned he had commanded my brother's company at West Point, one year behind me, although I hadn't known him. That gave us a bond and we talked on. Then, for no apparent reason, R.J. raised the subject of his wife's Christian faith and disclosed she had received the baptism with the Holy Spirit, with the manifestation of tongues.

That immediately got my attention. "Have *you?*" I asked him.

"No," he replied cautiously, and I sensed he regretted having told me about Mary Ann.

I turned to her. "Praise the Lord," I said. "I understand we have something in common."

We talked through dinner and well into the evening, thoroughly excited over our common experiences.

The next day, after chapel services, we joined the Wootens for brunch at their home, and I knew the Lord was nudging me toward R.J. I pressed ahead with my own experience of the baptism and the change in my life and ministry, and I showed him the scriptural support for the experience. I didn't back off, and asked him directly if he wanted to receive the baptism. I could see Mary Ann out of the corner of my eye, holding her breath, but silent.

"Yes, I'd like that," R.J. said after a slight pause.

We knelt in their living room, and he received the baptism readily, speaking in tongues fluently and bathing in happiness.

That experience drew us into a close relationship, and for the next year and a half R.J. and I met every morning for a half-hour of Bible study before going to physical training. We covered the entire New Testament and both grew immensely.

Another officer and his wife came to our home one night. Before long I was telling them about the baptism in the Spirit, but unlike R.J. they were turned off. They loved Jesus and desperately wanted more of Him, but their minds were closed to the baptism.

A few nights later, she was especially unhappy over the lack of joy and love in their home. She knew power was available, but seemed unable to grab hold of it. Walking into the kitchen alone, she began to pray and in a few moments reached the limit of expression in her language. And without realizing it, she began to speak with the language of God as the Spirit interceded with "groanings which cannot be uttered" (Rom. 8:26). She had stepped toward Jesus and he had baptized her with the Holy Spirit.

Unfortunately, her husband sank deeper into despair. His job got him down and he went all the way to the bottom; he became very sick. I went to visit him, and we prayed together. Three days later he was up, and they both came to my office. Again, I shared my Holy Spirit experiences with him, but he wanted nothing to do with the baptism. I felt there was nothing more I could do.

I was totally surprised two nights later when a knock came at the door and I opened it to find them standing there. A grin covered his face, and he almost shouted, "I want to be baptized with the Holy Spirit!"

I stood rather stupidly for a moment or two, not knowing what to say. But I gathered my senses and invited them in. They sat on the couch and told me how God, through the Scriptures, had convinced him the baptism was a real experience. They were on their way to a party, so without wasting time, we knelt in our living room and he received the baptism with the Spirit, with tongues and all, in a matter of minutes. What a new man! From despair and defeat to life and victory in nothing flat! They went off into the night to their party. They had a lot to talk about.

Within several weeks, the Lord began to move with miracles among the older families at the post. Two women were healed of badly deteriorating eyesight. One woman was healed of arthritis and a disease that was causing her body to reject her kidney. Several people were delivered from Satan's grip, and many more were cleansed of habitual sins and failures.

The Lord moved in particular in one family to bring a strong witness to His power throughout the whole community. It was the family of Bill and Wanda Miller and their five-year-old son, Billy. The boy was constantly afflicted with stomach aches that lasted for days at a time. No medication seemed to help.

I went to their house one night and into the boy's bedroom. "Hi, Billy," I said. "I've come to talk to you about your stomach aches." He was silent. "I want to get you to ask Jesus to heal you. He loves you, and He can heal you."

More silence. "I don't want to," he said weakly. I could see he was adamant, and I let it go.

I suggested to Wanda and Bill that they gently encourage Billy to ask Jesus for help. He steadfastly refused until several afternoons later the pain got so intense that he became desperate and, according to his later account, he sobbed, "Jesus, please help me!"

He was instantly healed, and his stubbornness vanished, too. A short time later, when another member of the family was ill, Billy immediately declared that Jesus could heal him.

Billy's healing raised faith in the household to the point where Wanda herself was healed. She had suffered from headaches and allergies since childhood. When we prayed, the headaches left, but the allergies persisted. At times she could hardly breathe, particularly as the cottonwood trees sent thousands of fluffy, cottonlike balls floating through the air. They nearly finished her.

Wanda continued to take allergy shots, but each time she took one, her body reacted. And that was worse than the allergy itself. The doctor cut the dose, but still she reacted. Finally, I told her God might be telling her to trust Him, and Him alone. "He often uses doctors to heal," I said, "but maybe He's trying to show you something special. But let Him tell you. Don't do it just on my word."

She prayed about it and, in a gigantic step of faith, stopped the medication. In a week, she was completely free. I laughed happily with her the afternoon we were outside and the fluffy cotton balls were filling the air. They were all around us, and Wanda merely flung her arms into the air and threw her head back. "I really am free!" she sang.

And that's the way it went. God was moving among young and old alike. He was doing something with us.

I wasn't certain when it began, but over those weeks in Germany I developed a longing to see the body of Christ functioning in all its power and variety within our community. I later learned that this longing was growing simultaneously in other Christians around the world, particularly in civilian life. It was a yearning to see Ephesians 4 fulfilled, a yearning to see the church really working, with all its members using the gifts they had been given, laity and clergy alike.

. . . When he ascended up on high, he . . . gave gifts unto men . . . And he gave some, apostles; and some, prophets; and some, evangelists; and some, pastors and teachers; for the perfecting of the saints, for the work of the ministry, for the edifying of the body of Christ; till we all come in the unity of the faith, and of the knowledge of the Son of God, unto a perfect man, unto the measure of the stature of the fulness of Christ . . . (vv. 8, 11-13).

I was beginning to perceive that the Lord had given us a very special situation there in Germany. We had exceptional variety, which we hadn't fully learned to handle yet, but we had extraordinary unity in our growing love of Christ. I sensed that that love of Jesus was going to spill over soon into an unprecedented love of brother for brother. I sensed that community, which was growing among Christians in amazing ways in the United States, was going to become a reality to us. We called ourselves a community; I felt we might actually become one.

One night at our Jesus Rally, a prophecy came through one of the people that stirred all of these yearnings within me and seemed to pull them together. "You have been growing and learning, and you are my people," the prophecy said. "From this moment on, things will never be the same among you. You will see new and startling things."

We were experiencing salvation; we were entering the life in the Spirit; we were seeing wonderful healings; we were seeing families restored. I knew in my spirit that night that the "new things" ahead for us would center on the development of the functioning, ministering body of Christ.

It was especially significant, too—with the benefit of hindsight—that as the spiritual surge was set in motion, things began to happen in my own walk with the Lord. The change began slowly and did not actually reach any measure of fulfillment for many months, even years, but I know it affected my own condition and was useful to the Lord in what He was doing with our community.

Without a doubt the most neglected area of my life, and I am confident this is the case with thousands of ministers, was my personal relationship with God. I had seen Him do signs and wonders and all manner of miracles, and He had often used me in performing them; and there was no question about my commitment to Him. I *knew* Him. But I had been negligent in some areas and I knew that such negligence was a source of weakness in many ministries.

I began to understand my own condition one evening when I listened to a tape by Jamie Buckingham, the pastor and author. I played it softly in the family room so as not to bother Nancy and the girls, lying back on the couch and lifting my feet up to the coffee table.

Jamie's voice was rather high-pitched and it rose even more with his enthusiasm. And he was enthusiastic about his central point on that tape—the necessity for learning the difference between "important" things and "urgent" things. "We spend so much time taking care of *urgent* things in our lives," he said, "that we never get around to the *important* things."

Jamie went on to use the case of a missionary in Indonesia as an illustration. It seemed that a writer in the United States went to Indonesia to investigate reports of "signs and wonders" connected with a major revival there. Someone told him about a missionary who had been involved in that revival. After a long, tedious journey by motor vehicle, boat, mule, and foot, the reporter finally arrived at the missionary's home. He knocked on the door; the man's wife answered. "Ma'am," he said, "I'm a newsman from the United States. I've traveled all these miles to talk to your husband about what God is doing here, and—" She stopped him and politely said, "I'm sorry; this is Monday, and Monday is my husband's day of prayer. You'll have to come back another day." And so the reporter went to the nearest village, spent the night, and returned the following day to get his story.

"Thank God," said Jamie, "for a man who was taking care of the *important* things and let the *urgent* things come as they would."

The tape ended, and I lay still on the couch. It had spoken directly to me. I was spending my life taking care of the "urgent" matters and never getting to the "important" ones. I answered calls of distress, ran here, ran there. Maybe I prayed and had devotions if I could work it in.

"I've got to do something about this, Lord," I said into the stillness of the room.

A short time later, I read a book on *The Christian Family* by Larry Christenson. In one chapter deep into the book he told about Martin Luther's daily prayer life. Normally Luther prayed two hours each morning, but when he faced an especially busy day, he set aside four hours. "Four hours!" I said it out loud. "How can this be?"

But I already knew something about the prayer life of other men of God. Wesley, Knox, Edwards, Finney, Wilkerson— they all were known to pray for hours each day.

It was nighttime. I knew the Lord was nudging me. I knew it because He had put the desire in my heart. I would get up early in the morning and take two hours for prayer. I winced. That meant setting the alarm for four-thirty A.M.

"Lord," I said to myself—Nancy was already in bed—"I'm not going to make a vow because I'm afraid I'll break it, but I do want to make an *appointment* with you. I'm making an *appointment* and I ask you to help me keep it."

He did. And it was invigorating—at first. But before long, I was having to fight to keep awake. In fact, there were times when I fell asleep. But I'd rouse myself, splash cold water on my face, and go back to my appointment. It worked. Indeed, it worked so well that I soon set my alarm for three-thirty so I could spend three hours with the Lord.

All my Christian life, the idea of such discipline had been almost repugnant. It was too dogmatic, too legalistic. Surely I should be able to pray when the Spirit moved me, and not have to enter into such regulation. But as I stepped into this realm, I was conscious of how natural laws had governed my experience. Nothing had been easy for me. Playing football had required tremendous effort and rigorous practice. Going to school had demanded hard study. The airborne and the ranger schools had pulled from me the very best I had to give.

Also, in the Scriptures I found the prophets in the Old Testament, and the disciples in the New, had paid a price. I had tried to convince myself that no price was required, and that was true for the gift of salvation. But I had been badly mistaken in applying this to my desire to follow Jesus. It's noteworthy that the words "disciple" and "discipline" have a common root.

A lot of my appointment with God was spent praying in tongues; a lot praying in English for specific things; a lot worshiping and adoring the Lord. I also began to read regularly from the Bible and then meditate on what I had read.

About a month after beginning my appointments, I was put to the test when the family and I took a vacation in the Netherlands. We camped, and each day brought below-freezing temperatures, snow and rain, and high winds. It was terrible. And I responded by lying in the sleeping bag every morning, too lazy to get up and have my appointment with the Lord. I can't remember a time when I was more miserable. I came apart. I was short-tempered with Nancy and the girls, and happiness eluded me entirely—all because I'd canceled my appointment with God.

I eventually shared my experiences with the body of Christ in Wurzburg, and the results were powerful. Many of them immediately saw that they spent their time keeping appointments with parents, teachers, doctors, lawyers, and businessmen. Why not with the Creator? Quite properly, they entered into variations. What was right for me was not necessarily perfect for them. I told them to adopt what they could handle, whether it was ten minutes or four hours, but to be faithful in it.

God was doing things in us.

The Sunday school was improving and attendance was beginning to rise. The choir was singing at every service and was excellent. We had a strong Bible study group, and it was growing. The Jesus rallies were getting bigger, up to fifty or sixty. But they were rowdier than ever, and many of the older folks couldn't cope with them. In fact, I knew that the Lord was becoming displeased with us over this. It was divisive. But more important than eliminating divisiveness was the need to develop worship throughout the community, the kind that would touch not only the young soldiers, but also the officers and the noncoms, the older, more traditional folks. The Jesus rallies were aimed right, but were not solidly on track.

The Lord began to show me, too, that the great emphasis on the coffeehouse ministry was diminishing, that He was going to do other things. As I prayed, I felt they would center on worship—corporate worship—the drawing together of the body.

My conviction reached the point one weekend where I proposed to several of the Christians, especially those showing leadership potential in the Thursday night meetings, that we meet to discuss worship and to study chapter fourteen of first Corinthians and its teaching on decency and order in prayer meetings. I invited them to our home.

Two nights later, forty of them jammed into the living room of our second-floor apartment. We were packed out, and happily with young and old, enlisted men and officers.

"Folks," I said, sitting erect in my easy chair, "I believe the Lord wants us to take a good, honest look at the matter of decency and order, particularly as it would apply to us."

Everybody was serious-faced, yet eager. I continued, "So, let's begin by reading 1 Corinthians: 14. And then let's talk about it."

It became immediately clear, at least to several, that we had been getting a little excessive and abusive in our meetings. We had, in fact, been rowdy, and this might be displeasing to the head of the church, the Lord. We had violated at one time or another, almost all of Paul's instructions on how the gifts of the Spirit—especially tongues and prophecy—should operate in a meeting. We had often babbled on and on in tongues, without proper interpretation, and we had run wild oftentimes with one prophecy after another, while the Apostle recommended that only two or three prophets speak. The results had not been edifying.

"But chaplain—" It was one of the young men. "Chaplain Vaughan, I hear you, but I also know that we're admonished not to quench the Spirit, and I feel that if you start laying down all sorts of rules and regulations, you're just going to quench everything."

Several nodded their heads vigorously, and there were several "amens."

I jumped in. "I agree that that's the last thing we want to do—quench the Spirit. And this poses a real tension for us. But I do believe we have entered into some excessive emotionalism and confusion in some of our meetings that is not in accord with what God wants us to do. For example, I'm sure that when some of the unbelievers have come into some of our gatherings, with people praying in tongues and shouting at the top of their voices, they must have thought us mad, just as Paul warns about in verse 23 here."

Several smiled weakly and looked at the floor.

Gradually a consensus emerged, and by praying and openly loving one another right there, we arrived at a better understanding of where we were and where we should be going. We were going to have to respect the authority of the leaders to call us to task if we got out of order.

After more than an hour of hard discussion, one of the older men spoke up. "This is good stuff. I believe we're moving forward, and I'm all for it. We want what God wants for us."

He paused and looked around the room. "But don't you think we ought to get ourselves together a little more so we can practice some of these things, these gifts and this worship, better than we have? I'm talking about a community-wide prayer and praise meeting, a worship meeting, on Sunday nights. Let's start a Sunday night service and open it up to the whole church and put these things into operation."

There were no dissenting voices.

That was late May of 1974, and late spring is no time to begin anything like a worship service. The army is no better than civilian life; everything connected with church dies in the summer. It was a fact that had broken my heart year after year. Nonetheless, we agreed to go ahead.

It was our first Sunday evening, and I wasn't sure what to expect. The chapel seemed nearly half full. I began to count by sections and in round numbers. We had more than a hundred and fifty people! Word had spread quickly.

The guitars led us into one of my favorite songs, "Thy Lovingkindness," and I watched the young people down in front sing joyfully. And my eyes roamed over the whole congregation. It was great—young people, old people, kids, all kinds of people. Half of them had their hands raised in worship. Many eyes were closed. "Thy lovingkindness is better than life. . . ." They sang it beautifully. Overnight we had improved our worship in song significantly.

We worshiped for forty-five minutes and then prayed for all kinds of needs both within and outside our community. Everyone prayed. Gone were the days when the chaplain alone addressed the Lord in public! And two people, a man and a woman, spoke prophetically about the increase the Lord was going to bring in the harvest and the preparation of workers for that job.

George was a major. At our third Sunday night service—a comfortable June evening—more than two hundred people had arrived when George approached me as we were ready to begin singing.

"Curry," he said, "I want you to pray for David, my son."

I was dumbfounded, and didn't say anything for several seconds. David was blind in one eye and just barely able to see out of the other. He had been born that way and was then five years old.

"Oh, man," I said to myself. "Lord, I'm not ready for this!" What could I say?

"Sure, brother," I heard myself replying. "We'll pray for him during the service."

"Good. Praise God." George returned to his wife, Janet, and the little boy. The child wore heavy, thick glasses. The three of them sat near the front.

I hadn't planned it, but early in the worship, I asked a small, pretty, young woman of Latin-American descent, whom I hadn't seen in our services before, to come forward and tell what God had done in her life. She told about the miraculous healing of her eye infirmity in recent weeks. The disease had caused progressive blindness.

"I just asked the Lord to heal my eyes, and I trusted Him, and He healed me, instantly," she said softly with a slight Spanish accent. "I believe He wants to heal us all."

As she sat down I said, "Well, is everybody's faith built up now? We didn't plan any of this ahead of time, but we're going to pray tonight for the healing of little David's eyes. You know him. His parents have asked us to pray for him."

A hush fell over the room. Everyone seemed to be holding his breath. George came forward, gripping the little boy's hand, and they knelt at the altar. The congregation spontaneously moved, surrounding them, laying hands on little David and on one another.

I prayed briefly. "Lord, you know all about this, and you know we don't have any power in ourselves to do anything about it. So we ask you, in Jesus' name, to heal David's eyes. Heal him, so he can serve you better, Lord."

Two or three others prayed similarly. It was a very tender few minutes. As the people returned to their seats, David and his father continued kneeling at the altar, and I went ahead with the meeting. We sang and prayed and worshiped. But David and his father were still there. "Why don't they go sit down?" I thought. I could see Janet watching them carefully.

We had agreed to have communion that night, so I started that part of the service. As the cup was going around, I noticed George taking a New Testament from his breast pocket. He held it in front of David and pointed at several pages. The boy's head nodded. Meanwhile, the singing rose higher and higher as we experienced the joy of the communion service.

In just a few moments, George got up and walked over to me. I leaned forward. "Curry, he can see!"

I looked into his face. It was wet with tears, and his eyes shone brightly. I looked over at the boy. He was watching me, and a smile broke across his face. I held my arms up and the singing dropped off sharply. I shouted, "He can see!" I waved my arms wildly. "This child has been healed!"

A wave of shouting, joyful and spontaneous, swept across the congregation. Every arm in the place shot up and worship—some in singing, some in shouting, some in weeping—rolled back and forth across the room. I had never seen anything like it. This, right in the middle of communion, was almost too much to handle.

The following morning, George and Janet took David to the hospital. The doctor looked puzzled as he spoke to the parents. "Well, medically speaking, it's impossible that he can see. The scar tissue from the damage he received at birth is still there."

George, excited, interrupted, "Doctor, please, no diagnosis. Just tell me: Can he see?"

The doctor paused, looked at the floor, and then looked up. "He can see."

Later, during a more thorough examination, the same doctor said David had perfect 20/20 vision in the eye for which he had worn a corrective lense and 20/25 vision in the eye that had one day earlier been sightless. This was recorded in David's medical record right along with the statement that he had been blind in one eye at birth.

News of the miracle of David swept across the city. In days, everyone seemed to be talking about "those charismatics." We went in short order from being a little Jesus party on Thursday night that no one ever heard of to being a church that prayed for the sick and saw them healed. In just a matter of weeks, our Sunday night attendance shot up to fill the church and rarely dropped below two hundred. Large numbers were accepting Christ, and many were going on to receive the baptism with the Holy Spirit. We even had people coming from the surrounding

German community.

Other miracles, healings, and deliverances followed in quick succession, and the church of Wurzburg seemed firmly established.

But there was more to it than the miracles and healings. In fact, not all in our growing community could technically be labeled "charismatics." They loved the Lord and were thoroughly committed to Him and His church, but they did not experience the manifestations of the Spirit in the same manner as the so-called charismatics. The one thing that was making us a real community, charismatics and noncharismatics together, was our growing awareness that God had brought us together, and was teaching us to love one another. "That's the secret, isn't it, Lord?" I said one night in prayer. "It's not just the miracles. It's the power of love." I was suddenly overwhelmed with a sense of that power—the power of love. "But it has to be lived out, hasn't it, Lord? It has to be expressed. You've called us together to express it."

I had been praying in my chair, and I dropped onto my knees. "Lord Jesus, this is what we must do. I beg you, Lord, show us how to do it. Lead us into it. We can't do it without you. Apart from you we can do nothing. Make us your real church—a real community of your people. Show us how to do it."

In September, a fellow chaplain, Colonel Peter Lent, approached me one afternoon. "Curry, your fellowship has really taken off. God's doing a terrific thing. But, you know, I fear it might get too big, even, and never get personal enough. I don't think you've even begun to minister the way the Lord wants you to."

He paused. I looked at him. His words seemed to echo my

168

thoughts of recent weeks.

"Why don't you start some small groups within the larger one?" he continued. "You know, small groups meeting in people's homes. They could get to know one another better and perhaps get a little deeper."

I knew he was right on the mark. This was what we needed.

But I moved slowly; I had no experience. I talked to the people Sunday nights; I met with groups of them in homes. "If we keep going the traditional way," I told them, "we'll have the traditional situation—one chaplain or pastor trying to minister to five hundred people. It's impossible. This can't be the way God wants His church to go. Smaller groups may be the answer. They don't cut into our larger meetings; they're additional. They provide for more detailed ministry and fellowship."

So, we started, with six groups, and left everything sort of loose. Some would emphasize Bible study; some would lean more toward prayer. But we began. Each group had eight to twelve people in it.

We must have touched the right key because we grew quickly. First six groups, then eight, then ten, then as many as sixteen, scattered all over Wurzburg.

The most amazing thing to me was watching the leaders for these groups be identified. It seemed that a guy would start to mature and show signs of leadership quality. He usually didn't see this in himself right away, but others did. Then, just as though a light bulb had gone on, he would see it himself. And there would be a full witness of the Spirit among everyone that so-and-so was a leader with pastoral qualities. The Lord plainly separated out those people whom He wanted to be leaders.

One interesting aspect of the selections was that we ended up with a lieutenant colonel, three majors, a captain, three sergeants, and two privates—almost the whole spectrum—in our early group of leaders.

I met with these men every Saturday morning for at least two hours. We talked about the progress of the individual groups, how problems were being met, what others should watch out for. I sometimes taught from the Scriptures.

This meeting was followed immediately by one of all the men in the community, which was more of a teaching meeting. The women of the community met similarly on Wednesdays. Then there were the Sunday school, the Sunday morning service, and the Sunday night prayer and praise meeting. This wide schedule provided for ministry on just about every level, from the small ten- or twelve-member groups all the way up through the full community service. This was good, for there were people who still kept pretty much to tradition, and preferred regular Sunday worship and maybe Sunday school to the more encompassing body-of-Christ life of most of the charismatics. This way, our charismatics and noncharismatics functioned well together; no one felt left out or threatened. And Jesus was the Lord of all.

God gave me a strong word early in our move into small group meetings. I shared it with the leaders on Saturday morning. "You guys are the leaders of the small groups God is leading us into. Each of you is the authority in your group, just as the husband should be the authority in the home. But let me give you a strong warning: If you want to lead, you must serve. You must be yielding, not brittle. You must love—and, more than that, you must learn how to live that love."

I paused. I wasn't sure it was sinking in, but I knew it had to. The Lord was speaking, not I. "Hey folks!" I almost shouted to the little group. Several of them jumped, and I smiled. I mustn't get harsh myself. "I really want you to hear this: Don't abuse people; just love them. You're servants. And you can't serve rightly without first loving."

It was several years before I heard about the abuses some of the other communities apparently fell into, particularly in the United States, in establishing small cell groups. I heard stories about overzealous leaders, obviously immature ones, who did great harm to people with their dictatorial conduct. And I heard tales about hierarchical structures from one city to another—"translocal authority," they called it—and alleged extremes involving money. I was so grateful to God that He shielded us from all that. We had our problems, usually in the category of learning how to love one another and how to refuse to gossip about one another, but I never found any abuses of the kind reportedly experienced elsewhere.

Instead I found people were actually able to get involved with other people in the love of Christ. I found the church could flourish in the manner in which the New Testament church seemed to have flourished. And this didn't involve only the superficial things, such as hugging and greeting one another in the way of the charismatic renewal generally. It penetrated into the pocketbook, into private property, into private time.

I remember the first Sunday night that we prayed for a family's difficult financial situation. The family wasn't begging; it was only asking the church to pray. After the meeting, I saw a man approach the head of the family. He reached out his hand. "Here, brother, Jesus laid it on my heart to give this to you." It was fifty dollars.

That was the beginning. People started learning how to share their lives as well as their prayer and praise.

Then came the time when one of the small groups was unable to handle a financial problem of a member. It was too big and complicated. After praying and talking among themselves at their weeknight meeting, they presented the problem to the community at large on Sunday. The problem, which involved a substantial sum of money, was solved that day. That, to me, was the New Testament pattern, and it still worked.

On another occasion, I saw one of our small groups fast and pray for one of its women members for deliverance and healing for sixty hours without interruption. The woman was delivered and healed. That, too, seemed to be the New Testament pattern.

Then the Lord, who surprised even the most experienced of us with his ability to run His own church, began to raise up other kinds of ministries, first within the small groups, and then within the larger body. It followed right along with the pattern of Ephesians 4:11-16 and 1 Corinthians 12:27-31. Quite unexpectedly, we would look up one day and there obviously was a person the Lord had called as a prophet. The person knew it, and the body of Christ knew it. This happened with all of the offices of ministry. The Lord was building *His* church.

One of the valuable lessons for me through this experience of God's bringing forth a community of His people—in the army, in Germany—was that man cannot build the church. God has to do it. He *can*, and He *will*. Teaching is not enough, although it is important. God must directly intercede and move in the hearts of people. The church then takes on a life and, since that life is the Spirit, it creates more life. It directly changes lives.

God loves the church. Only His Son was loved more.

11

FIRES IN EUROPE

I woke at four o'clock the morning of the conference. "Praise the Lord," I said to myself, getting up quietly so as not to disturb Nancy. "This will give me some time with the Lord before I go for John."

"John" was John Poole, the preacher from Philadelphia. He was to be one of our main speakers. Jamie Buckingham and his wife, Jackie, had already arrived.

The first traces of daylight were showing when I looked out the window. My breathing stopped. Snow was coming down by the tons. It looked like a blizzard. And we hadn't had enough snow that winter—the winter of 1975-76—to even mention. But here it was, February—the day of Reach Out '76, which had kept us on the rim of anxiety for eight months—and the heavens had turned loose. We were expecting people from all over Europe. Now what?

By midmorning the snow was still falling hard, and the telephones began to ring. The conference leaders were jammed into my office. "What do we tell the people?" I said, as the calls mounted. "Is God wiping this thing out right before our eyes?"

We stopped, and stood still before the Lord, all twenty of us. Some prayed aloud, but softly. In six or seven minutes I was convinced. "Listen, you guys," I said, my enthusiasm returning, "we believe God ordained this conference, don't we? If we really do believe that, we can only go ahead. Let's go right on through this thing."

I swung to the fellows nearest the phones. "Tell the people to come on! We're going to have a conference."

Every head in the room seemed to be nodding. "Lord, we believe." I heard the sentence repeated several times. A smile broke over Jamie's face as he said it. Then he said it again, louder.

"Praise God!" we shouted in unison.

"Praise God for the day and the blizzard and the conference," someone added.

The winter's worst snowstorm notwithstanding, fourteen hundred people swarmed into historic St. John's Lutheran Church in Wurzburg. They came from everywhere—military people, American civilians working abroad, German citizens, spiritually hungry people from all over western Europe. The fires of Christian renewal were well lighted.

The setting was perfect. We were the Lord's people, and suspended high above the breathtakingly stark altar of St. John's Church was a gigantic sculpture of the glorified Lord, seated, as though presiding over us, with a trumpet-sounding angel on each side. His hand was raised, and His lips parted. As I looked in wonder, I could almost hear the word from His lips—"peace." The excited and loving gathering—young, old, male, female, black, white—filled the main floor and two balconies. They were wearing everything from overalls to dress suits.

Reach Out '76 was our second such conference. The first,

Reach Out '75, had been held in Munich, attracting about eight hundred people. I had been called upon to help organize it, but the main sponsor had been Christian Books Unlimited. This year, our community at Wurzburg had carried the main load, under the auspices of the Chaplain's Office of the United States Army in Europe. The VII Army Corps had provided the funding.

We had gotten our feet wet in '75; this year, we jumped all the way in. And the people came with reports from all over Europe of renewal breaking out in army chapels, on military bases, in home prayer groups, and in the German communities themselves.

This drove right to the center of what I believed God was doing, not only among us at Wurzburg, but all over Europe, and all over the world. As I had prayed about our community's renewal, the realization came clearly that the American army was one of God's major missionary instruments. It provided one indirect way for Americans to help spread the gospel, even though they might not realize it. There was scarcely a household in the United States that did not have some contact, however tenuous, with the military forces. And if the Christians could reach the American military forces in Europe and around the earth with the gospel, their influence on others could be more far-reaching than any single body of men and women in the world.

I believe my thesis was reinforced at one point during the conference. It was at one of our afternoon meetings. "I want you to do something for me," I said to the people assembled. About twelve hundred of the fourteen hundred were present at that moment. "I want all of those who have received Christ since joining the military to stand."

It took several seconds for my request to sink in. Then slowly, they began to rise. All over the hall, people moved. Finally, at least half of the people were standing.

"One more minute," I said, while I had their attention. "Those of you who have found the Lord just since coming to Europe, raise your hands."

A majority of those standing lifted their hands. "God has been moving in Europe," I said with a chuckle, turning the meeting over to the speakers.

Jerry Curry was a brigadier general, a black man, and at forty-three, one of the youngest generals in the army. He was one of our evening testimony speakers at the three-day conference, and one of our most impressive, speaking from a position of authority and knowledge but of extraordinary humility.

"Just as important as defending the peace and maintaining the balance of power against the Soviet forces," he said, supporting my developing thesis, "is the task of spreading the gospel of Christ by the U.S. military personnel to the citizens of Europe. Thousands of those in the military forces, people just like yourselves, are really missionaries for Jesus Christ."

He spoke excitedly about the move of the Holy Spirit among the American troops. And the Lord's grace, he said with a grin, was even being felt among such unlikely people as colonels and lieutenant colonels. "In five years, if Jesus doesn't return first, there will be many Spirit-filled generals and admirals in the U.S. military forces," he declared to the ringing applause of his delighted audience.

As with General Haines years earlier, I was deeply touched as I watched this unusually talented general officer, who was to become deputy commander of the Military District in Washington and then a division commander, standing up openly for Christ. He was a real professional, one of his country's outstanding soldiers, but his faith came first. I knew beyond doubt that if someone walked up to General Curry and said, "Jerry, either deny Christ or you're out of the army," he'd say, "Well, I'm sorry but, praise God, I guess I'm out of the army."

Jerry Curry, married and the father of four, was one of those unusual people who, without presumption or piety, was able to say, "Looking back on my life, I can't think of a day when in my heart I wasn't a Christian." He made no effort to convey any holier-than-thou record of successful Christian living. But, as he matter-of-factly wrote later, he had believed the gospel all of his life. At the age of twelve, he had joined the Baptist Church—"a meaningful experience that I did not enter into lightly"—and had continued in Christian fellowship ever since.

But his life took a sharp turn in 1970 when, bound from Germany to his second tour in Vietnam, he stopped off in McKeesport, Pennsylvania, to visit his parents. His mother was the one who pointed the way for the turn when she abruptly asked one day, "How would you like to become the kind of Christian you think you are?" That shocking question set in motion a detailed discussion of the baptism with the Holy Spirit that culminated in his wife and daughter's receiving the baptism that very day and Jerry himself a week later. His three other children were subsequently similarly baptized.

"What a change it made in our family relationships!" the general said. "What a change it made in my military career! What a change it made in my relationship with God, my understanding of Him and His directives."

Writing for the *Military Chaplains' Review* in 1977, Jerry told of this turning point in his Christian life:

> Reading the Bible became a joy, where it had once been a chore. Understanding what God was saying became easy, where it had once been difficult. Applying what God was saying became difficult, where it had once seemed easy.
>
> There was no longer a conflict between me and

Satan, or between me and evil; that conflict had been resolved for all time. Jesus had triumphed over sin, death, hell, and Satan. Now the conflict was between me and God. Would I be obedient to His directives and become a co-worker with Jesus? Or would I stubbornly rebel, do my own thing, and become a co-worker with Satan? Warring within me were Jesus' obedience to God the Father posited against Satan's rebellion. The struggle goes on. But since I have been baptized with the Holy Spirit, I can joyfully say: "Christ is winning!"

Brigadier General Jerry Curry was just one additional solid example of the unusual thing God seemed to be doing with American military people. And the Lord gave us many more during our three days in 1976.

One of the most moving examples came near the end of one of our afternoon meetings. Jamie Buckingham finished his message and started to return to his seat, then stopped and bowed his head slightly, raised his clasped fingers to his chin in an attitude of prayer. He then turned to the microphone, and the crowd hushed. "Brethren, I believe the Lord wants us to turn to Him right now. He doesn't want any of us leaving here this afternoon without knowing Him, without having our needs met."

I could see people all over the sanctuary beginning to pray silently. Jamie continued: "I want all those who have not fully accepted Jesus Christ as Lord to come down to the altar and receive Him. And all of you who have not been baptized in the Holy Spirit, and want to be, you come on, too. The Lord wants to bless you."

The flood began. More than four hundred people of all descriptions filed to the altar, filling the area, some kneeling, some standing with arms outstretched, some weeping, some laughing and singing. I was aware that a significant number were from the two hundred or more attending the conference from the German community. Here was that chain reaction: The military people were being blessed, and they in turn were blessing others. I was also keenly aware that most of the ministry at the altar was being done by the nonprofessionals, the laymen. They came forward to lay on hands, counsel, and pray for those in need. Privates prayed for colonels, Germans prayed for Americans, and, in several cases, infantry officers prayed for chaplains.

After more than an hour of ministry, there was a spontaneous explosion of joy as many of the soldiers and some of the German citizens linked arms and began dancing around the altar. Someone produced a bongo drum. Tambourines appeared. Arm in arm, the men and women danced up and down the aisles, around the altar, and through the pews of the ancient church. It was like Jericho all over again, and the walls of the enemy came tumbling down.

In Wurzburg that February of 1976, we saw the hand of God moving powerfully. But before that climax could be reached, many doors had been opened, many fields plowed, and much sweat expended. And if one were to retrace the steps leading to that exciting celebration in the Lord, he would ultimately find himself face to face in many instances with Jim Ammerman, a colonel, a senior chaplain, a Southern Baptist, a man ministering to the body of Christ wherever he found it.

As I've said, our Reach Out '76 had been preceded by Reach Out '75 in Munich. But there had been many other events opening the way for the Spirit of God to move so publicly, and the moving force behind many of them had been Colonel E.H. Ammerman. In my view, he was used as much as any individual in opening up channels that had not theretofore been available for the charismatic renewal.

At that time, tall, lanky Jim was the V Corps chaplain, one of the three top chaplain's jobs in Germany. Although I'd heard of him while in school at Fort Hamilton, I first encountered him in the winter of 1973 at a conference for chaplains in beautiful Berchtesgaden in the East Bavarian Alps. Nearly one hundred and fifty chaplains were there. One morning he announced in his surprisingly deep, rich voice that there would be a meeting later that day for those interested in the charismatic movement. Twenty chaplains showed up, including me, and the teaching and encouragement were remarkable. Just his presence there as senior chaplain seemed to set the younger men free.

And there was the time at Frankfurt when he invited chaplains and troops from all over Germany to come to a meeting at the Post Chapel, which turned out to be an open, charismatic-style conference, really the first of the outreach kind of meeting. It was also the first ecumenical meeting of that sort, including Roman Catholics, Lutherans, Presbyterians, Baptists, independents, everyone.

And that's the way it went. So much credit for what seemed to be a burgeoning renewal in Germany and other parts of Europe had to go to Ammerman and others like him. He was solid, respectable, and learned, yet free, talkative, enthusiastic, and spiritual. He was a man who, unlike me at certain stages of my life, could get things done without ever letting them spin out of control. Many of us learned many things from him, exemplified by the words of wisdom he set down for the *Military Chaplain's Review* in its special issue on "The Charismatics":

> In most cases . . . I discovered that when I, a Southern Baptist, became as open to charismatics as I was to members of established denominations, my chapel was awarded with a most dedicated, zealous, and selfless new dimension of Christian worker. As

time went on, I further discovered that, while on the surface there appeared to be only about two to five per cent charismatics in the communities I served, actually there were many more. Originally I only knew about the most outspoken charismatics, those who were a bit abrasive to me and others. Nearly four times that many turned out to be charismatic. They included those who simply appeared to me to be warm, concerned, dedicated Christians. I was further enlightened to find that committed, volunteer chapel workers included nearly twice as many charismatics as other Christians. That percentage has held constant (or increased) in my last six assignments. . . . In most cases, they are the most genuinely ecumenical people I have ever known. Unfortunately, their sincere love is often misunderstood. If indeed they have made a renewed commitment to God and Christ, then they have further opened their hearts and lives for a new fullness of God. In a sense, there is more of God in them personally than before. God, who is Love, manifests himself in the individual by leading him to become more loving and tolerant. This is especially true of those whom I had not recognized to be charismatic for some time. I had only known them as loving, warm, dedicated Christians who loved me and cared for me. They voluntarily worked for me while I was being cautious, if not critical, of a phenomenon they had experienced. . . .

One of the primary doctrines of the Bible, unfortunately ignored, played down, or slighted, is the Lordship of Jesus Christ. Charismatics often make more of this than other Christians. Their understanding of the Lordship of Jesus involves every facet of life—time, talents, resources of money, position, and influence. Think what that type of dedication and submission to the Lord can mean in our military communities, in our chapel programs, in our financial needs and our voluntary requirements!

The great majority of charismatic Christians whom I have known have been a tremendous asset to our military Christian communities. They have a current, vital, and dynamic sense of the reality of the Christian faith. The Bible to them is a testimony of God's contemporary activity. Prayer is a joyful experience and is practiced much each day. Fellowship of believers (*koinonia*) under the Holy Spirit is a reality. Their ecumenism flows from a spiritual unity that transcends denominationalism. The Eucharist has a vital, fresh meaning of the Lord's Real Presence. The Christian faith is so precious, so joyful, that it is shared as a living experience. They overflow with the living Jesus and are adorned with an evangelistic fragrance. Their desire to be present with the Lord Jesus Christ renews the eschatological hope.

Acting from a position of ignorance or unconcern is shortchanging the kingdom. One chaplain even asked me how I "controlled" charismatics; did I have a special place for them to meet where they could "talk in tongues." My reply was that we had no special meetings. On our post we meet as Christians—Christians of differing spiritual warmth, position, and stance, yet all members of the body of Christ, each accepting the other as our physical bodies accept their various parts. Charismatics are a part of the whole, and I am one with them!

Understanding like that was paving the way for unprecedented Christian renewal in the United States Army.

12

FROM SEA
TO SHINING SEA

I had played on the streets and fields of Fort Leavenworth, on the Kansas banks of the Missouri River, as a child. My father was stationed there. Twenty-five years later I returned with my children for an unexpected tour of duty. I was to attend during the 1976-77 year the Army's Command and General Staff College, a school reserved for those who are expected to move on to the higher echelons of command. "What's a Spirit-filled chaplain being sent to a place like that for?" I wondered the day I was told of my assignment. The only answer I could come up with was: "The Lord must know what He's doing."

Fort Leavenworth, exaggeratedly infamous for the prison there, is a beautiful, historic military installation set in the heartland of America. Because of its limited purpose, it is comparatively small and very tight and neat. Except for the staff and faculty, people are assigned there for one year and then moved off to other parts of the world. It's further distinctive in that all the people are officers and their families.

I was slightly dismayed over once again being removed from the ministerial firing line, as I had been at Fort Hamilton, but the struggle was eased by the fantastic amount of Christian activity I encountered my first week on the post in mid-July. Things were happening. And, of course, who was behind a lot of it but my old friend from Germany, Jim Ammerman. He was the post chaplain.

Just before leaving Germany, he had shared a vision with me: twenty Bible studies going on all over Fort Leavenworth. The vision soon became reality. When I arrived, there were twenty-two study groups meeting every week, and before the year was out that figure rose to thirty. Just as it was in Germany, people were seeking Christ together in small groups during the week, then coming together on Sundays in celebration of what they were finding.

It took me about two weeks to realize that Ammerman, assisted by some outstanding laymen, was leading the most exciting and dynamic ministry in the military. People were finding Christ, growing in Him, and then going out into the world to tell about it. Soldiers really did make great missionaries!

The key to the Fort Leavenworth renewal was the Bible studies, directed under the post chaplain by George Kuykendahl, a lieutenant colonel who probably forfeited promotion to remain on the staff at Leavenworth and work with the ministry. Since retired, he was a serious-minded, but joyful intellectual completing his doctorate in counseling while at the same time giving untold hours to people. He cared, and it showed.

George had a scheme that worked. He insisted that when a study group grew to twelve members it had to split into two groups of six, and work up again. Each group had a coordinator, a study leader, and a host. No one person necessarily filled all three jobs. The coordinator stayed the same, but the other jobs rotated.

Because of the tremendous pressure the officers were under from the school, George set a rigid rule that the studies would not exceed an hour—usually consisting of ten or fifteen minutes of sharing and singing, and forty-five minutes or so of study. One minute was left for a closing prayer, and that was it. People who had to leave did so; the others could remain for fellowship and refreshments.

Each group had an eleven-month life, and it had to be brisk. The best we could hope for was, in most cases, an introduction of the people to the Scriptures and then to the person of Jesus Christ—although occasionally it happened the other way around. The Holy Spirit did all the work.

George, who was head of the Officer's Christian Fellowship at Leavenworth, a longtime moving force behind Christian activity in the military, met with the coordinators once a week, half of them on Monday for sharing and briefing, and the second half on Tuesday.

I was amazed when I discovered that half of the fourteen couples in our immediate neighborhood were participating in the Bible studies. And, just as in Wurzburg, the Christian life didn't stop with the small groups. A strong Sunday school program was flourishing at the chapel, and I was grateful for a chance to help with the teaching. And then, the regular Sunday congregation rarely dropped below seven hundred for both services. All told, it appeared that forty per cent of the population at Fort Leavenworth were participating in the Christian life to one degree or another, which was astounding in view of trends in civilian life. It appeared to me that more than half of those participating in the chapel program were charismatic Christians, too, which was doubly astounding.

One extremely powerful activity was the once-a-month prayer meeting at Jim Ammerman's home on Saturday night. We called it an all-night prayer meeting; actually, it began at eight P.M. and ran till two or later in the morning, until all the needs and intercessions had been taken care of. One night fairly early in my year there, I dropped in on the meeting. As we prayed for one another and for every kind of intercession imaginable, one lady, the wife of an officer, began one of the most moving confessions I'd heard.

"Look at me. I'm an officer's wife, from a good army family, 'good folks,' everyone says, but they only see me on the outside. They don't know the real me."

She sobbed miserably, and it was difficult to understand some of her words. "I beat my children," she cried. "I brutalize them. I beat them awfully." Her face was in her hands. "They'd lock me up if they knew what I did to my children. I scream at them. I curse them. I hit them. I'm not fit to be a mother."

The group rallied to her and began to pray, seeking discernment on how to minister to her. The problem obviously was old and deep-rooted. Before long, it was apparent to all that Satan had her in bondage in several areas of her life. We began to rebuke the devil, and the Lord quickly delivered her; she was thoroughly freed that night. The ministry, under Ammerman's oversight, was quiet and gentle, and extraordinarily effective.

Interestingly enough, the very next day, one of the woman's children was healed of incapacitating hay fever.

It was early in the study year at Fort Leavenworth. Our first guest speaker was the man who had commanded Americans held prisoner of war in North Vietnam. Today he is a major general in the air force.

The general, a slender but forceful man, walked to the head of the auditorium and began to talk to us about his experiences as a prisoner of war. As with General Haines, General Curry, and so many others, his lecture took on unusual depth as he wove in his own Christian testimony and the need for faith in situations such as those the POWs found themselves in. "Those without faith didn't do so well," he said simply. "Indeed, most of them did not make it."

He drove the point home in several ways, and each made an impact. I watched the men in the class carefully. "The Lord was there, even in that prison camp," the general declared. "All we had to do was perceive it."

As with General Haines, it was difficult to say precisely how the POW hero's remarks were received by each individual. But there was clearly an impact. I saw one colonel approach George Kuykendahl and say, "George, I want to talk to you." That's all I heard, but that was enough. They went to George's office, and the colonel accepted Christ that afternoon. Other results were purely between the Lord and the individuals.

After I graduated from West Point, the Officer's Christian Fellowship traditionally sponsored a Bible study on every post. But, frankly, it usually operated in something of a corner, very sincere, but little known. And there were the traditional chapel activities, usually struggling along gamely over in another little corner. Most of the enthusiastic Christians went off downtown where the civilians often had something a little livelier going on.

But today this has begun to swing the other way. Christian activity is stirring at most posts around the country and overseas, too. Where there was one O.C.F. group, there now may be five. Where there was no charismatic activity, there now is something of this nature on most posts. Where the chapel services were impersonal and sterile, they now are warm and active. And now the people are adding the dimension of meeting in their homes and in small, closely knit groups elsewhere.

The Lord is clearly moving among the American military.

It's not always a flashy movement, but it's a steady one. It reminds me of the beat of a drum; it just keeps going on. And people keep marching steadily, more and more joining the ranks.

God is very patient, and He's worked patience in a lot of the men He's used in this renewal. He's taught us to wait—to trust and rest, just continuing to talk about Him and the Holy Spirit. Usually whatever happens in civilian society eventually works its way into the military. There's often some lag, but it happens. When the society is restless, the military grows restless. When Vietnam was boiling in the sixties, with public opinion roaring and youth rebelling, the same attitudes penetrated the military. When drug abuse ripped through society, it ripped through the military. When God began to awaken the general population to Jesus and the Holy Spirit, He soon started stirring up the soldiers and sailors. Now renewal is everywhere.

It's interesting that God didn't wait until the second half of the twentieth centruy to start touching soldiers. Jesus moved among them from the very beginning of His ministry, and the apostles continued.

I've always been impressed by the fact that it was a soldier—a centurion—whom Jesus described as a man having faith exceeding any He'd found in Israel (Matt. 8:5-10). And it was a centurion who testified at the foot of the cross that Jesus truly was the Son of God (Matt. 27:54) and a righteous man (Luke 23:47). And, of course, God chose a centurion, Cornelius, and his household as the first gentiles to be visited with the Holy Spirit (Acts 10).

Throughout the Old Testament, we find God using soldiers and warriors frequently, David being the most obvious example. He was Israel's greatest warrior and yet was a man after God's own heart.

When men all over the world have talked to me about the profession of soldiering in relation to their love of God and desire to follow Him, I have pointed out that in none of these cases did the Lord tell the centurions and warriors to lay down their arms and quit being soldiers. I think that is significant. It shows the Lord of the universe knows far better than anyone that as long as there are fallen men and corruption and hate there will be a need for armies. How good it would be for a nation to have an army of God's people!

General Curry has said it forcefully: "God intends that Christians not only make the military a career, but when they go to war they are to fight better than unbelievers. The Christian's action in combat should be an inspiration to others. His deeds on the field of battle should be as heroic as Jonathan's or King David's. . . . From Genesis to Revelation, God's attitude toward war is unchanging. God elected, elects, and will continue to elect to use war as an instrument to accomplish His purpose whenever His divine wisdom requires it. God is not, nor will He be, anti-war. . . . The conclusion of Revelation pictures Jesus himself returning as the last general, the last commander in chief personally directing war against rebellious, earthly governments and their armies."

I am grateful to God for allowing me to see His working among the United States Army and other branches of the military. I am convinced that we are in the midst of the greatest Christian revival the services have known. All of us owe a great debt of gratitude to the men God chose to become instruments of blessing and mercy in the early days of this revival, only some of whom have been mentioned in this account.

Where would I have turned without Bob Crick and Merlin Carothers, for example?

Bob has continued to be one of the finest chaplains I have known—a Church of God minister, director of the Clinical Pastoral Education Center at Fort Benning, Georgia, and a man with a heart for souls. He has been more instrumental than anyone I know in bridging gaps from time to time between the traditional pentecostals and the neo-pentecostals or charismatics. "To old and new pentecostals alike," he wrote in the *Military Chaplains' Review*, "this movement cannot be interpreted on narrow pentecostal themes (tongues, prophecy, healing, discernment of spirits, etc.), but must be seen in the larger sense of God's total involvement in church, ministry, and the world. The sources of its strength in the military have been experienced in a resurgence of teaching, preaching and general acceptance of the 'real' presence of God in and through the Holy Spirit."

Merlin, meanwhile, has been used by the Lord in multiple careers. He served the military with extraordinary effectiveness in the fifties and sixties and was instrumental in leading many people into the fullness of the Spirit, including myself. In the early seventies, he retired from the military, having been used by God to launch one of the most revolutionary waves to touch the charismatic renewal. His books on praise, beginning with *Prison to Praise*, gave the renewal, both in civilian life and in the military, an unprecedented shot forward that is still felt today.

General Haines was one of the most effective Christian witnesses in the army until his retirement in 1973. Since then, he has continued to minister within the military establishment but has broadened his horizons to reach into many corners of American civilian life. He has ministered powerfully within his own denomination, the Episcopal Church, and has crisscrossed the country—and other nations, too—to carry the gospel and the reality of life in the Holy Spirit to any who are interested.

General Curry, meanwhile, takes the good news of Christ wherever he goes to serve the army and has been one of the leading speakers at major Christian conferences in the society at large, including those of the Full Gospel Business Men's Fellowship International.

Jim Ammerman, after a career of dynamic Christian ministry that touched multitudes on several continents, has now retired to take up a teaching and conference ministry as a civilian. Untold numbers of people, within the military and outside, continue to be blessed by his very special gifts.

It is virtually impossible to name the people used by God in this renewal. The list seems endless, even touching on only a few of those I've known and served with:

Chaplain Dennis Brewer of the Air Force, retired.

Chaplain Dino Rogakos of the Army, Fort Lewis, Washington.

Lieutenant Colonel Rudy Ostovich of the Army, the Pentagon.

Major Bill Miller of the Army, the Pentagon.

Major Gene Cargile of the Army, the Pentagon.

Lieutenant Colonel Cal Tichenor of the Army, the Pentagon.

Major Robert Zeddeber of the Army, the Pentagon.

Major Chuck Krulak of the Marines, Okinawa.

Chaplain Billy T. Smith of the Army, Command and General Staff College, Fort Leavenworth.

Chaplain Thomas L. Deal of the Army, Command and General Staff College, Fort Leavenworth.

Lieutenant Colonel Dutch Kough of the Air Force, retired.

Colonel Doug Cartey of the Air Force, retired.

Lieutenant Colonel Joe Callahan of the Army, Germany.

Major Mel Case of the Army, Germany.

Major Joe Terry of West Point, a tactical officer.

Chaplain Doug Nelson of the Army, Germany.

Chaplain Don Hodson of the Army, Fort Hood, Texas.

Lieutenant Colonel Pete Deoss of the Army, Fort Hood.

Sergeant First Class Don Putz of the Army, Fort Lewis, Washington.

Sergeant First Class Bob Warner of the Army, Fort Stewart, Georgia.

Sergeant Randy Swope of the Army, Army Depot, Michigan.

Specialist 5 Roger Sapp of the Army, Fort Rucker, Alabama.

Lieutenant Colonel R.J. Wooten of the Army, Fort Polk, Louisiana.

Chaplain W.T. Permenter of the Army, Fort Polk, Louisiana.

Major H. Gwynn Vaughan of the Army, Fort Bragg, North Carolina.

Sergeant First Class George Wesley of the Army, Fort Stewart, Georgia.

Warrant Officer Donn Purcell of the Army, Fort Bragg, North Carolina.

Major General Clay Buckingham of the Army, the Pentagon.

General George Blanchard, commander, U.S. Army Forces in Europe.

Lietutenant General E.C. Meyer of the Army, deputy chief of staff, the Pentagon.

And that's the way it went.

And when Jesus was entered into Capernaum, there came unto him a centurion, beseeching him,
    And saying, Lord, my servant lieth at home sick of the palsy, grievously tormented.
    And Jesus saith unto him, I will come and heal him.

BATTLEGROUND

The centurion answered and said, Lord, I am not worthy that thou shouldest come under my roof: but speak the word only, and my servant shall be healed.

For I am a man under authority, having soldiers under me: and I say to this man, Go, and he goeth; and to another, Come, and he cometh; and to my servant, Do this, and he doeth it.

When Jesus heard it, he marvelled, and said to them that followed, Verily I say unto you, I have not found so great faith, no, not in Israel.

—Matthew 8:5-10.

For further information, please address your correspondence to:
Chaplain (LTC) Curry N. Vaughan, Jr.
P.O. Box 1000
Montreat, North Carolina 28757

For free information on how to receive
the international magazine

LOGOS JOURNAL

with NATIONAL COURIER update
also Book Catalog

Write: Information - LOGOS JOURNAL CATALOG
Box 191
Plainfield, NJ 07061